G 8 Summit Trainer

Students' Workbook

Gymnasiale Oberstufe (G 8)

Herausgegeben von:
Prof. Dr. Engelbert Thaler

Erarbeitet von:
Dr. Michaela Banzhaf, Thomas Bohlen, Dr. Maria Eisenmann, Jochen Fritz, Martin Kohn, Carmen Mendez, Alexandra Peschel, Dr. Roland Petersohn, Prof. Dr. Engelbert Thaler, Thomas van Breda

Sprachliche Betreuung:
Simone Duxbury-Ziemer

Schöningh

Alle Materialien zu „Summit G8“ können über den Buchhandel oder direkt beim Verlag bezogen werden:

- Summit Schülerbuch, 368 S.
  Best.-Nr. 040035
- Summit CD-ROM – Abitur- und Klausurentrainer, 8 interaktive Klausuren
  Best.-Nr. 062411

  Zusatzkurse
  Best.-Nr. 062418

  Kostenloses Demo zum Download unter www.schoeningh-schulbuch.de/summit-demo
- Summit Audio-CDs mit Hörtexten und Songs, ca. 2 x 74 min
  Best.-Nr. 062399
- Summit Hörverstehen – Übungen, Tests, Abiturvorbereitung, ca. 104 S. inkl. Audio-CD u. CD-ROM
  Best.-Nr. 040029

www.schoeningh-schulbuch.de
Schöningh Verlag, Jühenplatz 1–3, 33098 Paderborn

Druck 5 4 3 2 1 / Jahr 2014 13 12 11 10
Die letzte Zahl bezeichnet das Jahr dieses Druckes.

Umschlaggestaltung: Nora Eumann, Bielefeld
Druck und Bindung: westermann druck GmbH, Braunschweig

ISBN 978-3-14-040036-7

Contents

Audio version on CD available

Use your exercise book

Stepping In

Summit G8, p. 10

1 Jokes

Language awareness

British humour often results from the broad variety of expressions, homophones (words with the same pronunciation, but a different spelling and meaning), homonyms (words with more meanings) and puns (plays on words).

a. Read the following jokes aloud to work out their meaning.

b. Explain the source of humour in these jokes.

c. Find two further jokes.

1. A giant of a man walked into a Dublin pub with a tiger on a lead. He looked grimly round the bar and then shouted at the barman, "Do you serve Englishmen in here?" "Of course, sir," said the nervous barman. "Good," said the man, "I'll have two for the tiger."

2. Why did the frankfurter turn red?
It saw the salad dressing.

3. Joe: Is that dog of yours a watchdog?
Jack: Yes.
Joe: Can he tell me the time?

4. Tim: Have you ever hunted bear?
Tom: No, I always hunt with my clothes on.

5. "I don't want you using those bad words any more."
"But, Mother, Shakespeare uses them."
"Well, don't play with him again."

Summit G8, p. 10

2 False Friends

Avoiding mistakes

Are they talking about the same thing? Obviously not. "gymnasium" is a so-called *false friend*. These are words that look and/or sound similar in English and German but differ in meaning.

Complete the following chart and add the missing words.

German	English	can be mistaken for ...
brav	well-behaved, good	brave – tapfer
	wallet	briefcase –
	boss	– *Koch*
Folie (f. OHP)		foil –
Mappe/Hefter		map –
Mörder		murder –
	mint	to mince –
mobben		– *der Pöbel*
Handy		handy –
	poison	
Lektüre		lecture –
	novel	Roman –
prägnant	concise	– *schwanger*
	staff, personnel	
Rezept (Verschreibung Arzt)		– *Rezept (Kochen)* – *Quittung*
Lyrik		– *Liedtexte*
Hose		hose –
Stoff (Textil)		stuff –
		tablet –
Wand		

Tracing National Identities – Cool Britannia and America Dreaming

Summit G8, p. 14

1 Britishness: What Does It Mean to You?

Vocabulary training

Revise your vocabulary. Link the words on the left with the corresponding definitions in the right-hand column.

1. expat	**a.** a type of thick cream
2. to conjure sth. up	**b.** a person living in a country that is not their own
3. self-effacement	**c.** to make sth. appear as a picture in your mind
4. to cling	**d.** to make a long cut with a sharp object
5. trait	**e.** desire to not attract attention to yourself or your abilities
6. subservient (to sb./sth.)	**f.** to hold on tightly to sb./sth.
7. to cane	**g.** a particular quality in your personality
8. to slash	**h.** an idea, a belief or an understanding of sth.
9. clotted cream	**i.** too willing to obey other people
10. indigenous	**j.** a small amount of strangeness
11. to detest	**k.** to hit a child with a cane as a punishment
12. notion	**l.** belonging to a particular place rather than coming to it from somewhere else
13. dash of eccentricity	**m.** to hate sb./sth. very much

Summit G8, p. 16

2 Rule Britannia

CD 1, 1

Vocabulary training

The lyrics of the song *Rule Britannia* were written by James Thomson in the first half of the 18th century. Therefore, it contains a number of words which are rarely used or not used at all today. This makes it difficult for modern readers to fully understand the text.

a. Look up the words and fill in the grid. Add more words you are unfamiliar with if necessary.

quote	modern English equivalent	quote	modern English equivalent
Heaven's command		shalt	
azure		dread	
main		thy	
charter		woe	
strain		thine	

Britons		renown	
blest		commerce	
thee		repair	
thou			

b. Use the grid to rewrite the song in a modern English prose text.

A Hanging

3 Summit G8, p. 17

Tense, aspect, voice

There are three categories according to which a conjugated verb is defined: its tense (present tense, past tense, present perfect, etc.), its aspect (simple, progressive), and its voice (active, passive). The form of a verb is chosen according to the situation in which it is used (e. g. if an action is happening at the present moment of speaking, the present progressive is used).

Fill in the following grid according to the following categories. Then search *A Hanging* for at least four more examples.

example from the text	tense, aspect, voice	explanation of usage
A sickly light, like yellow tinfoil **was slanting** over the high walls into the jail yard.	*past progressive, active voice*	*the action was in progress at the past moment of speaking; setting the background*
One prisoner **had been brought out** of his cell.		
[...], while others **handcuffed** him, **passed** a chain through his handcuffs and **fixed** it to their belts, and **lashed** his arms tight to his sides.		
The hangman **is waiting**.		
Suddenly, when we **had gone** ten yards, the procession **stopped short** without any order or warning.		
He walked clumsily with his bound arms, but quite steadily, with that bobbing gait of the Indian who never **straightens** his knees.		
And then when the noose **was fixed**, the prisoner **began** crying out on his god.		
Well sir, all **has passed off** with the utmost satisfactoriness.		

Summit G8, p. 23

4 Focus on Facts: From Empire to Commonwealth

Mind mapping

Arrange the following expressions in the mind maps below and complete them with ideas of your own.

Australia and New Zealand	world peace	human rights	British West Indies
largest empire in history	19th and early 20th centuries		free trade
framework of common values and goals	equality of women		

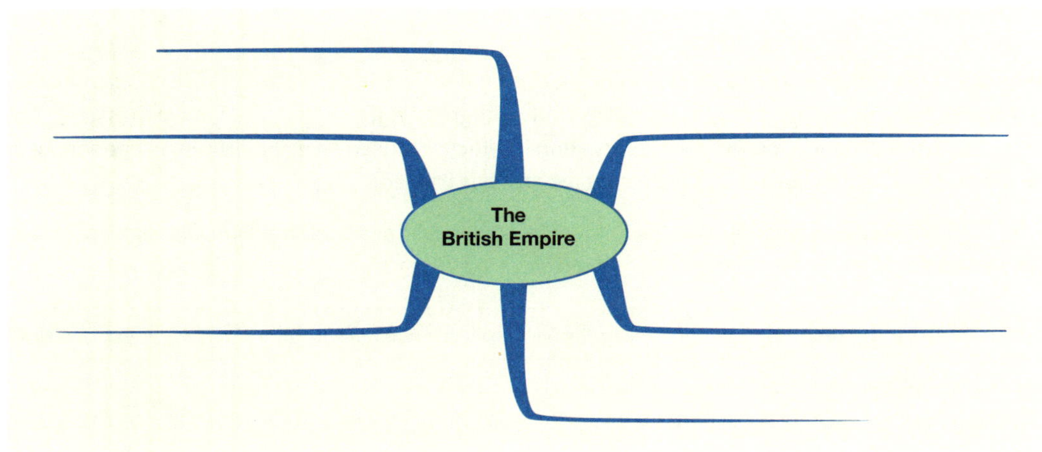

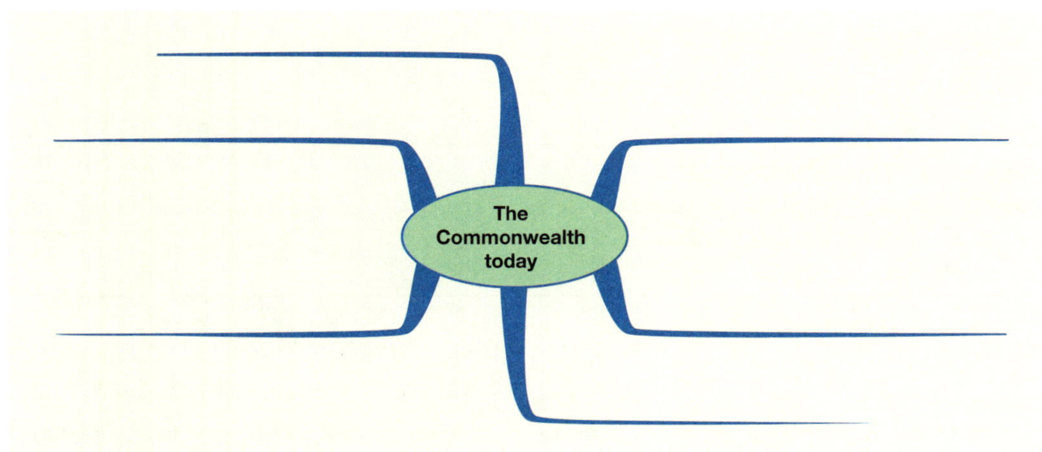

Summit G8, p. 26

5 Focus on Facts: British Core Values

Vocabulary training

a. The following passage describes the 'rules of the game' in England. Complete the text by filling in the following words and phrases in the correct order.

tennis	codify	heritage	Englishness	originated
essential part	popular	set of rules	athletic games	accident

Rules of the Game

It is no ______________________ **(1)** that almost all of the most ______________________ **(2)** sports and games played around the world today ______________________ **(3)** in England. Football, baseball, rugby, ______________________ **(4)** were all invented here, and even when we did not actually invent a sport or game, the English were usually the first to lay down a proper, official ______________________ **(5)** for it (hockey, horseracing, polo, swimming, rowing, boxing – and even skiing, for heaven's sake). And that's not counting all the rather less ______________________ **(6)** and pastimes such as darts, pool, billiards, cards, cribbage and skittles. And let's not forget hunting, shooting and fishing. We didn't create or ______________________ **(7)** all of these, of course, but sports and games are widely recognized as an ______________________ **(8)** of our culture, our ______________________ **(9)** and our legacy – one cannot talk about ______________________ **(10)** without talking about sports and games.

from *Watching the English. The Hidden Rules of English Behaviour* by Kate Fox, London, Hodder and Stoughton, p. 239

Mediating

b. Cribbage, skittles, polo: Research one of these fringe sports/games, and then explain its rules in German briefly. → Students' Book, Method Kit, p. 258

What Is an American?

6 Summit G8, p. 28

De Crèvecœur wrote about his ideas of the American, which you might have talked about in the lessons. Let's now take a closer look at the language he uses.

Word family

a. Find the corresponding adjectives for the following nouns and complete the grid.

noun	adjective	noun in German
posterity		
science		
vigour		
industry		
labour		
gratitude		

Rural America

b. Find the corresponding nouns for the adjectives given and fill in the grid below.

adjective	noun	adjective in German
equal		
strong		
exuberant		
despotic		
mighty		
voluntary		

Paraphrasing

c. Replace the phrases in bold type and change the sentence structure if necessary.

Example: He is an American who, leaving behind him all his ancient prejudices and manners, receives new ones from the new **mode of life he has embraced**, the new government he obeys, and **the new rank he holds**.

... manner of living he has eagerly chosen to pursue ... his new status in society

1 . He becomes an American **by being received** in the broad lap of our great Alma Mater.

____

____

2. The Americans were once scattered all over Europe; here they are incorporated into one of the finest systems of population which has ever appeared, and which **will hereafter become distinct** by the power of the different climates they inhabit.

____

____

3. Here **the rewards of his industry** follow with equal steps the progress of his labour; his labour is founded on the basis of nature, self-interest; can it want a stronger allurement?

____

____

4. Wives and children, **who before in vain demanded** of him a morsel of bread, now, fat and frolicsome, gladly help their father to clear those fields ....

____

____

5. The American is a new man, who acts upon new principles; he **must therefore entertain new ideas**, and form new opinions.

____

____

Summit G8, p. 33

7 Focus on Facts: American Core Values

Explanations

Explain the following phrases about various American core values in your own words.

1. from rags to riches
2. patriotism
3. optimism
4. social order
5. the pursuit of happiness
6. inalienable rights
7. the frontier
8. Puritan work ethic

Manifest Destiny

8 Summit G8, p. 33

Vocabulary training

The following text gives you information on an important key term of the American Dream – the concept of Manifest Destiny.

Read the text and fill in the gaps with the following words:

beliefs	concepts	culture	expansion	history
ideologie	liberty	torch	overspread	phenomenon
possess	Providence	ralling	simplest	tangible
territories	movement			

American history can be seen as a chronological record of events which are presented in history as being ________________ (1), often being tied to a date. The term Manifest Destiny, on the other hand, is a ________________ (2) which cannot be tied to a date, but rather existed and still exists as the philosophy that embraces American ________________ (3) as a whole. Manifest Destiny is an ________________ (4) that created American history. In its ________________ (5) form, Manifest Destiny can be defined as "A ________________ (6)." It is the body of ________________ (7) and ________________ (8) that forms American life and ________________ (9).

The movement was given its name in 1845 by democratic leader and influential editor John L. O'Sullivan, who, in an attempt to explain America's thirst for ________________ (10), and to present a defense for America's claim to new ________________ (11), wrote:

> "... the right of our manifest destiny to ________________ (12) and to ________________ (13) the whole of the continent which ________________ (14) has given us for the development of the great experiment of ________________ (15) and federative development of self-government entrusted to us. It is the right such as that of the tree to the space of air and the earth suitable for the full expansion of its principle and destiny of growth."

Manifest Destiny became the ________________ (16) cry throughout America and was publicized in the papers and advertised and argued by politicians throughout the nation. The Manifest Destiny became the ________________ (17) that lit the way for American expansion.

Summit G8, p. 38

9 How to Defeat Terrorism

9/11 deeply marked American history and policy. The author Fareed Zakaria from *Newsweek* argues that, instead of "closing the gates", the world needs an open, confident America as an alternative to a war-focused anti-terror policy.

Error spotting

There are two errors (word order, wrong word, spelling, article, tense, conjunction, preposition) in every line. Cross out the errors and write the correct version into the right-hand column.

Text with errors	Correction
We ~~never will~~ be able to prevent ~~the~~ small group of misfits from	will *never*; *a*
planing some terible act of terror. No matter how far-seeing	
and competent our intellegence and law-enforcment officials,	
peoples will always be able to slip throu the cracks in a large,	
open and diverse countrie. The real test from American	
leadership is not weather we can make 100 procent sure we	
prevent the attak, but rather how we response to it. Stephen	
Flynn, a homeland-security experte in the Council on Foreign	
Relations, argue that our goal should be resilience – how quick	
we can bounce back from a disruption? In the materiels	
sciences, he point out, resilience is the ability from a material to	
recover it's original shape after the deformation. If one day	
bombs do go of, we must ensure that they cause so little	
disruption – economical, social, political – how possible. This	
would deprive the terrorist from his main objective. If we will	
not be terrorized, than in a crucial sense we defeated terrorism.	
[...]	

From: Fareed Zakaria: Beyond Bush – what the world needs is an open confident America. In: *Newsweek*, June 11, 2007, pp. 22 ff.

Church Meets State

10 Summit G8, p. 45

Particles

The following text gives you information about Evangelicals in the USA. Read the text and write the appropriate prepositions or conjunctions in the gaps.

Southern Baptists, as a rule, do not drink. But once a month, young congregants ______ (1) the Journey, a Baptist church, and their friends get together ______ (2) the back room ______ (3) a sprawling brew pub called the Schlafly Bottleworks ______ (4) talk ______ (5) the big questions: the President, faith and war, the meaning ______ (6) life, and 'what's wrong ______ (7) religion.' 'That's where people are having their conversations ______ (8) things that matter,' the Reverend Darrin Patrick, senior pastor and founder ______ (9) the Journey, said ______ (10) the talks ______ (11) the bar. 'We go where people are because we feel like Jesus went ______ (12) the people.'

The Journey, a megachurch ______ (13) mostly younger Evangelicals, is representative ______ (14) a new generation that refuses ______ (15) put politics ______ (16) the center ______ (17) its faith and rejects identification ______ (18) the religious right. They say they are tired ______ (19) the culture wars. They say they want ______ (20) broaden the traditional Evangelical anti-abortion agenda ______ (21) include care ______ (22) the poor, the environment, immigrants and people ______ (23) H.I.V., according ______ (24) experts ______ (25) younger Evangelicals and the young people themselves.

from *Taking Their Faith, But Not Their Politics, to the People* by Neela Banerjee. In: *The New York Times*, June 1, 2008 (Beilage zur *Süddeutschen Zeitung*, June 16, 2008, p. 7)

Public Life and Political Culture

Summit G8, p. 50

1 Her Majesty and Her Subjects

Queen Elizabeth took part in a thanksgiving service for her 80th birthday. After she had left St. Paul's Cathedral, she met members of the public during one of her famous royal walkabouts.

Working with a photo

Describe the photograph, paying special attention to details like people's gestures or the expressions on their faces.
→ Students' Book, Method Kit, p. 285

Use some of the following words:

on the occasion of	Prince Philipp
elderly man	fence
bowing gesture	loyalty
subjects	

Summit G8, p. 54

2 How Much Britain Had Changed in 50 Years

In 2002, Queen Elizabeth II celebrated her Golden Jubilee. How much had Britain changed during her reign of 50 years? Study the statistics.

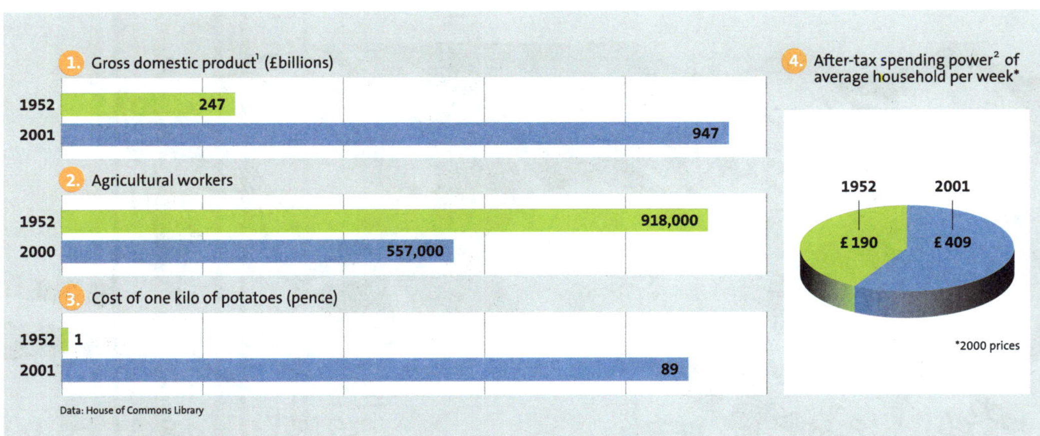

[1] **gross domestic product** *Bruttosozialprodukt* –
[2] **after-tax spending power** *Verdienst nach Steuern*

Analysing statistics

a. Put the missing words in the correct form into the following description of the statistics about the development of the economy in the UK.

agricultural	amount	bar chart	compared	doubled
incomes	indicate	occasion	pence	penny
pie chart	provides	published	rose	third
value				

The statistics given were published (1) in the magazine *Time* in 2002 on the ______ (2) of Queen Elizabeth's Golden Jubilee. The numbers show the change in Britain within the space of 50 years.

The first bar chart ______ (3) information about the total ______ (4) of all goods and services produced in the UK in 1952 ______ (5) to 2001. The ______ (6) rose from £ 247 billion to £ 947 billion. In contrast to this development, the number of agricultural workers as shown in the second ______ (7) decreased by more than a ______ (8), from 918,000 in 1952 to 557,000 in 2000. This number may reflect the ongoing change of the UK from an ______ (9) to an industrial and technological country. As the third chart shows, however, prices for agricultural products ______ (10) considerably in 50 years. Whereas one kilo of potatoes cost 1 ______ (11) in 1952, it cost 89 ______ (12) in 2001. The ______ (13) shows the development of people's after-tax spending power per week which more than ______ (14) in the time span investigated. The numbers ______ (15) that living costs increased more quickly than ______ (16).

b. Examine the following statistics about changes in society and describe them in a coherent text. Use the hints and vocabulary given in the → Students' Book, Method Kit, p. 284.

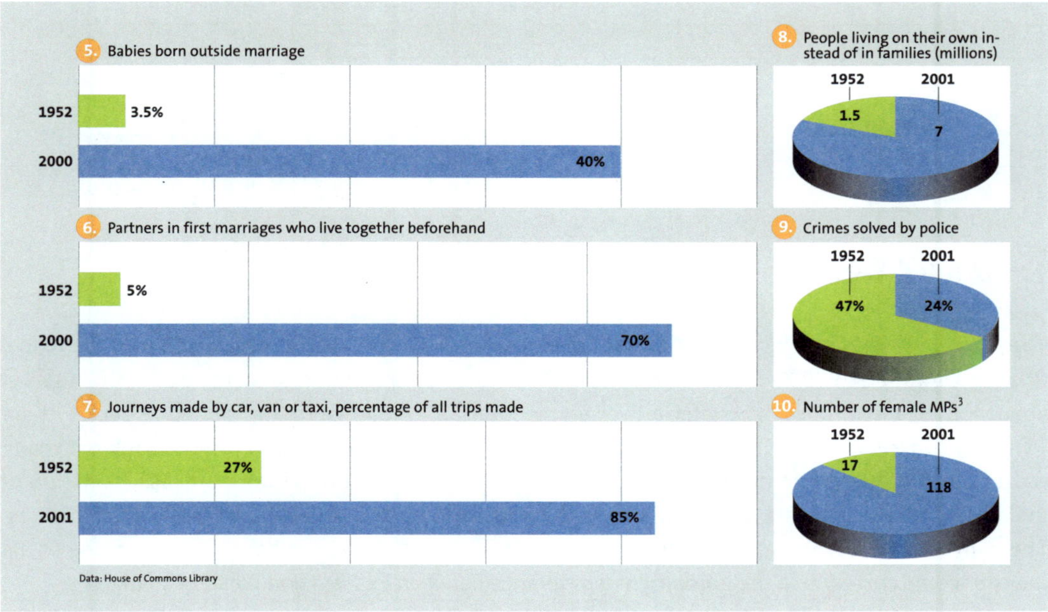

[3] **MP** Member of Parliament

c. Discuss whether the pie charts are an appropriate graphic presentation of the issues. Why might the TIME magazine have chosen this form instead of a bar chart?

Summit G8, p. 57

3 Focus on Facts: The Political System in the United Kingdom

Use the information from the *Focus on Facts* page to fill in the graph below.

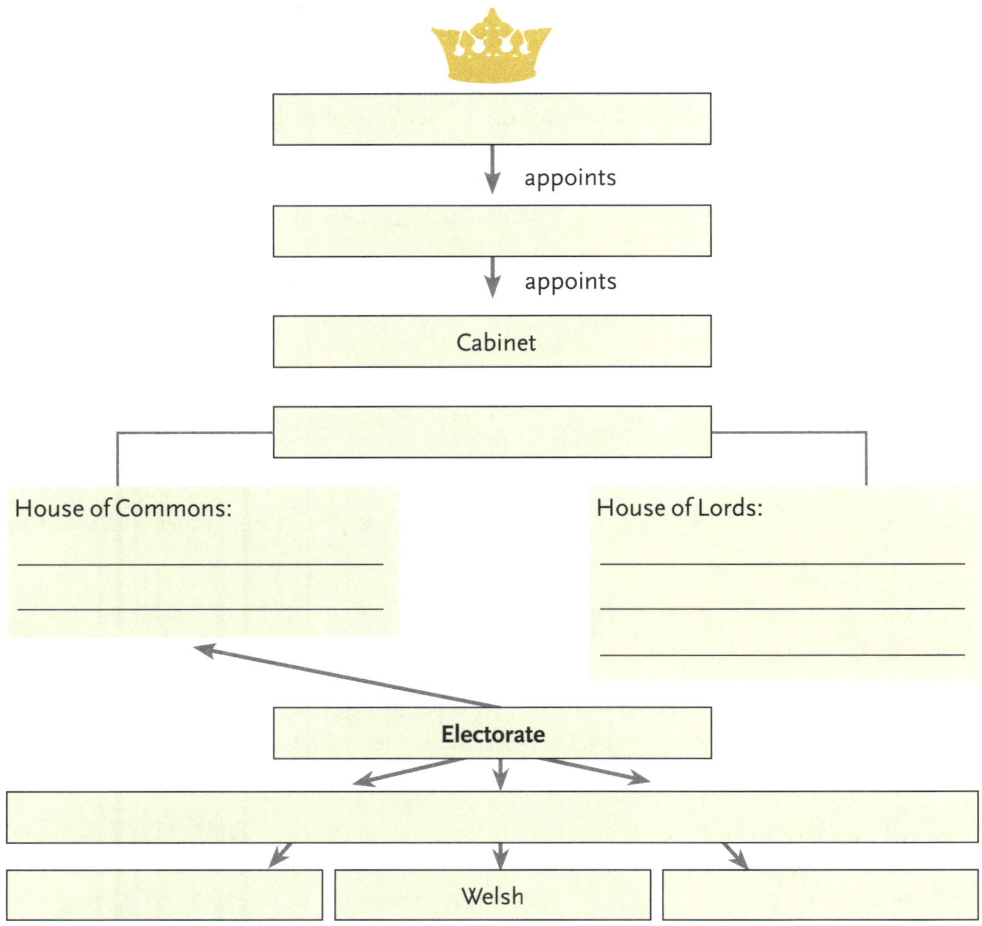

Summit G8, p. 59

4 Orhan Pamuk: Democracy and the Word of Allah

Orhan Pamuk

The following text is an extract from Orhan Pamuk's novel "Snow" (2002) which won him the Nobel Prize in Literature in 2006. It is the first Nobel Prize to be awarded to a Turkish citizen. The novel is about Ka, a Turkish poet, who after a twelve-year political exile in Germany has gone back to Kars ('snow' in Turkish), a Turkish town on the border to Armenia and Georgia, to find out what made young Muslim women commit suicide. He witnesses a military coup following the assassination of the director of the Institute of Education who had openly objected to religiously motivated suicides. The conversation between Ka and Blue, the representative of political Islam in Turkey, is one of his many encounters to grasp the fundamental difference between Eastern and Western thinking.

For a long tense moment, the two stared at each other.
"Yesterday you told me that you had every intention of writing about the suicide girls in the Western press," said Blue.
Remembering his little lie, Ka felt embarrassed.
"Which Western newspaper did you have in mind?" Blue now asked.
"At which of the German papers do you have contacts?"
"The *Frankfurter Rundschau,*" said Ka.
"Who?"
"It's a liberal German newspaper."
"What's his name?"

"Hans Hansen," Ka said, and hugged[1] his coat.

"I have a statement for Hans Hansen. I intend to speak up against the coup," said Blue. "We don't have much time. I want you to start writing it down this instant."

Ka opened to the back page of his poetry notebook and began to take notes. Blue began by saying that at least eighty people had been killed so far (the actual death toll, including those shot at the theater, was seventeen); numerous schools and houses had been raided[2] and tanks had destroyed nine shanties[3] (the real figure was four); after claiming that some students had died under torture, he alluded to some street skirmishes[4] that Ka had not heard anyone else mention; passing rather quickly over the sufferings of the Kurds, he slightly exaggerated those visited on the Islamists; it was, he now said, to provide a pretext for this coup that the state had arranged for the mayor and the director of the Institute of Education to be assassinated. The reason for all this, he said, was to prevent the Islamists from winning the elections. The banning of all political parties and associations proved his point, he said.

As he went into more detail, Ka looked straight into Kadife's[5] eyes; she hung on Blue's every word. In the margins of these pages he would later tear out of his poetry notebook, he made a number of drawings and doodles that proved he was thinking about Ipek[6]: a slender neck, a head of hair, a child's house with childish smoke rising out of a child's chimney ...

Many years before, Ka had explained to me that when a good poet is confronted with difficult facts that he knows to be true but also inimical[7] to poetry, he has no choice but to flee to the margins; it was, he said, this very retreat that allowed him to hear the hidden music that is the source of all art. Ka appreciated some of Blue's pronouncements enough to record them in his notebook word for word.

> Contrary to what the West seems to think, it is not poverty that brings us so close to God; it's the fact that no one is more curious than we are to find out why we are here on earth and what will happen to us in the next world.

Instead of explaining the source of this curiosity and revealing mankind's purpose on earth, Blue's final words posed a challenge to the West:

> Will the West, which takes democracy, its great invention, more seriously than the word of God, come out against this coup that has brought an end to democracy in Kars? [He stopped here to make a grand gesture.] Or are we to conclude that democracy, freedom, and human rights don't matter, that all the West wants is for the rest of the world to imitate them like monkeys? Can the West endure any democracy achieved by enemies who in no way resemble them? I have something to say to all the other nations that the West has left behind: Brothers, you're not alone.

He paused for a moment. "Can you be sure that your friend at the *Frankfurter Rundschau* is going to print all this?"

"He takes offense when people discuss the West as if it's a single person with a single point of view," Ka said carefully.

"But that's how it is," Blue said, after another pause. "There is, after all, only one West and only one Western point of view. And we take the opposite point of view."

"The fact remains that they don't live that way in the West," said Ka. "It's not as it is here; they don't want everyone thinking alike. Everyone, even the most ordinary grocer, feels compelled to boast of having his own personal views. If we used the term *Western democrats* instead of the West, you'd have a better chance of pricking people's consciences[8]."

"Fine, do what you think best. Must we make more corrections to get this published?"

"Although this began as a news item, it's become more interesting, more like a proclamation," said Ka. "They might want to put your name to it ... and maybe even include a few biographical details –"

"I've prepared those already," said Blue. "All they need say is that I'm one of the most prominent Islamists in Turkey and perhaps the entire Middle East."

"Hans Hansen is not going to print this as it stands."

---

[1] **to hug** to hold tightly – [2] **to raid** to attack – [3] **shanty** primitive hut – [4] **skirmish** ['skɜːmɪʃ] short military engagement – [5] **Khadife** the woman in love with Blue, Ipek's sister – [6] **Ipek** the woman in love with Ka – [7] **inimical** [ɪ'nɪmɪkl] harmful – [8] **to prick one's conscience** to stir your awareness of what is morally acceptable

"What?"

"If the social-democratic *Frankfurter Rundschau* were to print a statement from a single Turkish Islamist[9], it would seem as if they were taking sides," Ka said.

"I see. When something doesn't serve Mr. Hans Hansen's interests, he has a way of slithering away," said Blue. "What do we need to do to convince him?"

"Even if the German democrats come out against a military coup in Turkey – and it has to be a real coup, not a theatrical one – they'll still be very uneasy if the people they're defending are Islamists."

"Yes, these people are all terrified of us," said Blue.

Ka could not tell if he was boasting or merely feeling misunderstood.

"Well," he said, "if you included the signatures of a liberal ex-Communist and a Kurdish nationalist, you'd have no trouble getting this announcement into the *Frankfurter Rundschau*."

Orhan Pamuk: Snow. London, Faber & Faber, 2005, pp. 227–229

---

[9] **Turkish Islamist** believer insisting on the supremacy of Islamic law over secular state law instituted by Kemal Ataturk

Reading comprehension

a. Tick the correct answer. There is only one solution.

1. The main reason for the military coup was
- ☐ the death of some students under torture.
- ☐ an Islamic victory in the elections.
- ☐ the suffering of the Kurds.

2. When a good poet is confronted with difficult facts, he
- ☐ tries to hide them in his texts.
- ☐ hears music to find the source of his art.
- ☐ ignores them.

3. What brings Muslim people close to God according to Blue?
- ☐ poverty
- ☐ a desire for democracy
- ☐ the revelation of mankind's purpose on Earth

4. Under what condition will the German newspaper probably print Blue's article?
- ☐ if Blue's name and biographical information are given
- ☐ if there is more than a single point of view
- ☐ if the views of Western democrats are printed

5. How does Blue interpret Ka's explanations?
- ☐ He thinks the publisher will take sides.
- ☐ He states the publisher won't print the article.
- ☐ He supposes Western people are terrified of Muslims.

Text analysis

6. Which type of narrator does Pamuk use in the extract?
- ☐ first-person narrator
- ☐ third-person limited narrator
- ☐ third-person omniscient narrator

7. What is the intended effect of the point of view on the reader?
- ☐ The reader can easily identify with one of the characters.
- ☐ The reader can form his opinion on the two characters and their political attitudes quite objectively.
- ☐ The reader will be more interested in politics.

b. Match the following words and phrases from the text with their explanations.

Vocabulary

to feel embarrassed (l. 4)	to feel attacked
to allude to sth. (l. 18)	to recognize the good qualities
to provide a pretext for sth. (l. 20)	to feel forced
to appreciate sb./sth. (l. 31)	to mention sth. in an indirect way
to endure sth. (l. 42)	to give a false reason for doing sth.
to take offense of sth. (l. 47)	to feel awkward, shy or ashamed
to feel compelled to do sth. (l. 52)	to experience and deal with sth. that is unpleasant

c. Write a short statement in which you explain the difference between Eastern and Western thinking and views on the working of the press. Refer to the text.

Personal opinion

Focus on Facts: Milestones of Democracy

5 Summit G8, p. 61

Recalling knowledge

Study the *Focus on Facts* page in your Students' Book on p. 61 carefully. Then do the following tasks.

1. Name three sources that have contributed to the British constitution.
2. What rights did the Magna Carta ensure for the first time and when was it signed?
3. What does Habeas Corpus mean and what did the Act ensure?
4. Why do you think the Magna Carta and the Habeas Corpus Act are milestones of democracy?
5. What does a constitutional monarchy mean and when was it founded?
6. Recall three facts about the American Declaration of Independence.
7. Translate the following extract from the Declaration of Independence and explain its meaning: "They are endowed by their Creator with certain unalienable rights ... To secure these rights, Governments are instituted among Men, deriving their just powers from the consent of the governed."
8. Who wrote the American Declaration of Independence and the American Constitution and when were these documents written?
9. What does "amendment" mean in German?
10. Enumerate at least four rights ensured by the American Constitution and its amendments.

The first cabinet of the USA in 1789. President George Washington, Thomas Jefferson, Alexander Hamilton, Henry Knox and Edmond Randolph.

Summit G8, p. 62

6 An American Political Icon

Barack Obama has rapidly become a modern-day political icon. Another American who is still a political icon is Dr. Martin Luther King, a former leader of the Civil Rights Movement, who strictly opposed the use of violence as a means of resistance. For this reason, the American people were shocked when he was shot dead. Even years after his assassination, people can still remember this day clearly – just like the author of the following text.

Tense, aspect, voice

Put the verbs in the correct tense, aspect and voice.

I ______________________ (remember/**1**) that April evening so clearly. My father ______________________ (come/**2**) out of one of his upholstery shops[1] in suburban New Jersey when I ______________________ (walk/**3**) up to him. I ______________________ (just hear/**4**) the news on the radio and ________ (be/**5**) anxious to tell him.

"Martin Luther King got shot," I ______________________ (say/**6**).

An odd look ______________________ (cross/**7**) my old man's face, like he ______________________ (punch/**8**) unexpectedly and ______________________ (try/**9**) not to show that it ______________________ (hurt/**10**). "Where?" he ______________________ (ask/**11**).

It ______________________ (be/**12**) not a geography question. "In the head," I ______________________ (say/**13**).

My father ______________________ (turn/**14**) around and ______________________ (walk/**15**) back into the store.

Dr. King's message of peaceful change notwithstanding[2], there ________ (be/**16**) nothing more American than brutal violence. The country ______________________ (build/**17**) on it, ______________________ (revel/**18**) in it and ______________________ (show/**19**) every evidence of clinging to it with the crazed, destructive strength of an obsessive lover.

Dr. King ______________________ (understand/**20**) with unusual clarity the price to ______________________ (pay/**21**) for the terrible belief that every problem ______________________ (can/**22**) be settled by a bullet or a bomb. He ______________________ (warn/**23**) his followers and the nation as a whole to avoid the "quicksand"[3] of violence and hatred. He ______________________ (urge/**24**) blacks to remain nonviolent in the face of horrendous injustices, and he ______________________ (speak/**25**) out boldly against the war in Vietnam.

We ______________________ (honor/**26**) Dr. King, but we ______________________ (never listen/**27**) to him. Our addiction to the joy of violence ______________________ (be/**28**) far too strong. We ______________________ (go/**29**) to search like hollow-eyed junkies all day and all through the night for a rationale, any rationale, to keep the killing going. Democratic politicians ______________________ (suffer/**30**) for years because they ______________________ (be/**31**) insufficiently insistent on violence as a solution to national problems.

Abridged from: Bob Herbert: "An Obsession with Violence" from *The New York Times*, February 2, 2006

One means of peaceful resistance were sit-ins. Here, King is being arrested during a lunch counter sit-in, 1955.

[1]**upholstery shop** a shop where padded covers are put on furniture – [2]**notwithstanding** in spite of something – [3]**quicksand** deep wet sand that you sink into and cannot escape from, here: a metaphor for a vicious circle

Focus on Facts: The Political System in the USA

7 Summit G8, p. 68

Matching

a. The following text is about the process of campaigning in the USA: The phrases on the left are given in the right order. Match them with the jumbled phrases on the right so that the whole text makes sense. Prepositions and linking words will give you a clue. The solution to the first sentence is given.

1. Compared with the short political campaigns of other democracies,	1 i	**a.** is the ability to raise large sums of money, especially early on in the race.
2. Campaigns can start anywhere from several months		**b.** as mail-in ballots are a commonly-used voting method.
3. Candidates are often recruited		**c.** he or she will make a public announcement.
4. But these are often interested		**d.** to several years before election day.
5. During this period, candidates will consider their ability		**e.** and meet with voters; speaking to them in crowds, small groups, or even one-on-one.
6. Once a person decides to run,		**f.** in electing like-minded politicians.
7. This announcement could consist of anything		**g.** by political parties and interest groups.
8. One of the most important aspects of the American political campaign		**h.** at persuading voters to support the candidate.
9. Also during this period, candidates travel around the area		**i.** campaigns in the United States can be marathons.
10. Later, television, radio, and direct mail campaigns are launched, which are aimed		**j.** to put together the money, organization, and public image needed to get elected.
11. Voting in the United States often starts weeks before election day		**k.** one aimed at mail-in voters and one aimed at the more traditional poll voters.
12. That is why campaigns will often run two persuasion programs,		**l.** from a simple press release to a major media event followed by a speaking tour.

ing-forms

b. A considerable part of campaigning is done by grassroots political movements, whose work is described in the following text. Fill in the gaps with the suitable noun or gerund.

advertising	gathering	organizing	raising	talking
polling	putting	reminding	setting	transporting

A grassroots political movement is driven by the constituents of a community, which means by the ordinary people rather than a party. Grassroots movements organize and lobby through various procedures including: house parties and meetings, ________________ **(1)** up posters, ________________ **(2)** with pedestrians on the street, ________________ **(3)** signatures for petitions, ________________ **(4)** up information tables, ________________ **(5)** money from many small donors for political ________________ **(6)** or campaigns, ________________ **(7)** large demonstrations, ________________ **(8)** people to vote and/or ________________ **(9)** them to ________________ **(10)** places.

Barack Obama, elected 44th President of the USA, during his final campaign rally on Nov. 3, 2008

Summit G8, p. 70

8 The Contrapuntal Civilization

9 CD 1

The poem *The Contrapuntal Civilization* deals with two different faces of the American lifestyle.

Listening for verbs

a. Listen to the poem and fill in the missing verb forms.

1. I have ______________ in Vietnam.
But I have ______________ the face
of the moon.
2. I have ______________ the waters and
______________ the air of a
magnificent land. But I have ______________
______________ it safe from disease.
3. I have ______________ through the
sky faster than the sun.
But I have ______________ in streets
________ ugly with traffic.
4. I have______________ the land with
garbage.
But I have______________ upon it
a hundred million homes.
5. I have ______________ schools
with my prejudice.
But I have ______________ armies
to ______________ them.
6. I have ______________ down my enemies
with clubs.
But I have ______________ courtrooms
to ______________ them free.
7. I have ______________ a bomb
to ______________ the world.
But I have ______________ it
to ______________ a light.
8. I have ______________ my brothers
in the alleys of the ghetto.
But I have ______________
a human heart.
9. I have ______________ out
filth and pornography.
But I have ______________
the philosophy of man.
10. I have ______________ children
______________ from my golden towers.
But I have ______________ half of the earth.
11. I ______________
in a grotesque slum.
But I ______________ by
the silver spoon of opulence.
12. I ________ in the greatest country
in the world in the greatest time
in history. But I ________ the ground
I ________ upon.
13. I ________ ashamed.
But I ________ proud.
I ________ an American.

Anonymous: "The Contrapuntal Civilization" from *The Contrapuntal Civilization. Essays Toward a New Understanding of the American Experience*, ed. by Michael Kammen, New York, Crowell, 1971

Liberty through garbage?

b. Write down an additional stanza, taking the picture from above into consideration.

Creative writing

Focus on Facts: The Global Role of the USA

9 Summit G8, p. 72

Vocabulary training

The mind-map that has been started below describes the global role of the USA. Remembering what you have learnt in previous lessons, arrange the following words and phrases in the mind-map with the aim of giving a short presentation on the issue.

arms race | competition and open trade | social Darwinism | improvement of living conditions

dollar diplomacy | war on terror | human rights abuse | Iron Curtain | Manifest Destiny | WW I

promotion of peace, freedom, democracy and safety | world leadership | Iraq war | peace-keeping role

Monroe Doctrine | Cold War | no foreign entanglements | territorial expansion | puppet governments

foundation of NATO and UN | Truman Doctrine

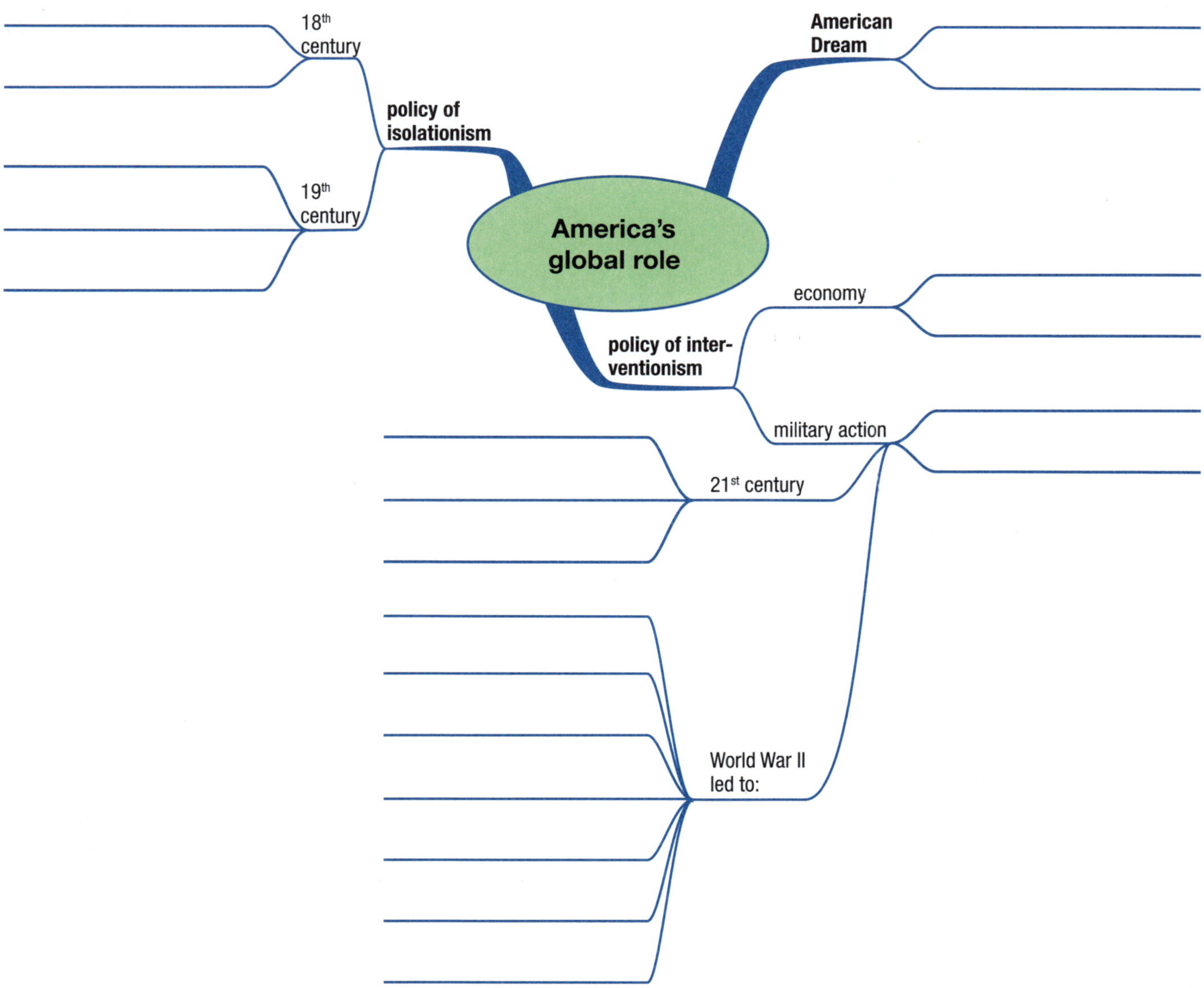

Summit G8, p. 74

10 Star Gazing

The photo "Star Gazing" is one of the latest works by the German artist Hans Haacke, who has been living in New York since 1965. Haacke is a representative of political conceptual art.

Working with a piece of art

a. Describe the photo (→ Method Kit, Working with visuals, p. 285) using the following words:

quadrangular hood | medium shot | cloth | dark blue | cover | enveloped head | US flag

The photo shows ______________________________

____

____

The hood is made of ______________________________ with

______________ and it stands for the ______________________________

The photo is taken as a ______________ but attention is mostly drawn

____

____

b. Analyse the photo using the following phrases:

violence | treat like animals | Iraq war | detention camps | soldiers | torture | symbol of | violation of human rights | prisoners | anti-terror policy

The image has to do with ______________________________

____

It refers to ______________________________

____

____

The photo alludes to ______________________________

The hood represents the USA and the red colour of the shirt may stand for ______________________________

____

The title has a double meaning. On the one hand, the word "star" represents ______________________________ and on the other hand, the title "Star Gazing" could also be understood as a criticism of ______________________________

____

____

____

c. Evaluate the photo:

The photo touches me because ______________________________

____

____

____

____

____

d. In what way can a flag be a symbol of freedom?

Rivals – Allies – Friends

Summit G8, p. 80

1 The United States, Germany and Europe: A Historian's Perspective

Vocabulary training and style

This is a student's weak summary of Junker's speech. Give the correct, more appropriate or less common alternatives for the words in bold type. Going through the speech in your Students' Book again will help you.

The author is ~~**very much worried**~~ _deeply concerned_ about the ~~**nowadays**~~ _current_ state of American-German relations, and about the ~~**high**~~ _growing_ anti-Americanism in Europe.

The **going-together** ________ (1) of Germany **made** ________ (2) **the highest-quality** ________ (3) Germany: a **middle** ________ (4), democratic country with **little** ________ (5) political influence and economic **meaning** ________ (6). The **people** ________ (7) of the **"old" Germany liked** ________ (8) freedom, democracy, **being rich and buying a lot** ________ (9) like no other generation before.

President Bush and Chancellor Kohl **said** ________ (10) that the two **countries** ________ (11) would become **equal bosses** ________ (12).

After 9/11 millions **met** ________ (13) at the fallen Berlin Wall to **show that they were sad** ________ (14). "Solidarity **without limits**" ________ (15) became the slogan of the Berlin government.

The Bush **government** ________ (16) is criticized because they **do not accept** ________ (17) international laws. American citizens have been **taken** ________ (18) and put into prison without having the right to a **jury** ________ (19), without being able to see **an advocate** ________ (20).

This is a **hurt** ________ (21) of human rights which has **very much** ________ (22) undermined US authority.

The author finishes the article with his **thinking** ________ (23) that no **big** ________ (24) problem in the world can be solved without the **working-together** ________ (25) of the old and the new world.

Summit G8, p. 83

2 "Warme Brüder und EU-nuchen"

The article "Anti-Europeanism in America" by the British historian Timothy Garton Ash was published in *Die Zeit* under the title "Warme Brüder und EU-nuchen". An extract from both texts is given here.

Mediation

Compare the German translation with the original. List at least one example from the text to exemplify the following translation techniques.
→ Students' Book, Method Kit, p. 258

1. Translating idiomatic phrases: their values and their spines – Werte; ____________

2. Use of fillers: in a word – sie sind halt; ____________

3. Change of word types and phrases: polities – politische Gebilde; ____________

4. Omission of information: ____________

5. Change of word order: ____________

6. Change of singular and plural: ____________

7. Change of passive into active sentences: ____________

8. Change of noun phrase into verbal phrase: ____________

9. Rendering participial constructions: ____________

10. Personal → impersonal: ____________

Anti-Europeanism in America	Warme Brüder und EU-nuchen
To the list of polities destined to slip down the *Eurinal* of history, we must add the European Union [...]	Auf die Liste der politischen Gebilde, die ausersehen sind, im Urinal der Geschichte runtergespült zu werden, müssen wir auch die Europäische Union [...] setzen [...]
Virtually everyone I spoke to on the East Coast agreed that there is a level of irritation with Europe and Europeans higher even than at the last memorable peak in the early 1980s. Pens are dipped in acid and lips curled to pillory "the Europeans", also known as "the Euros", "the Euroids", "the peens", or the "Euroweenies".	Wenn von Europa und den Europäern die Rede ist, kommt fast überall Gereiztheit auf. Sie übertrifft die letzte Verstimmung in den frühen Achtzigerjahren bei weitem. Um „die Europäer" oder auch „die Euros", die „Euroiden", die „Eurowürstchen" anzuprangern, taucht man die Schreibfedern in Säure.
The current stereotype of Europeans is easily summarized. Europeans are wimps. They are weak, petulant, hypocritical, disunited, duplicitous, sometimes anti-Semitic and often anti-American appeasers. In a word: "Euroweenies". Their values and their spines have dissolved in a lukewarm bath of multilateral, transnational, secular, and postmodern fudge. They spend their euros on wine, holidays, and bloated welfare states instead of on defense.	Europäer gelten als Weichlinge, schwach, querulantisch, heuchlerisch, zerstritten, zuweilen antisemitisch. Zu oft erweisen sie sich als antiamerikanische Beschwichtiger. Sie sind halt „Eurowürstchen". Sie haben ihre Werte in multilateralen, transnationalen, säkularen und postmodernen Spielereien verloren. Statt für Verteidigung geben sie ihre Euros für Wein, Urlaub und aufgeblähte Wohlfahrtsstaaten aus.

Anti-Europeanism in America	Warme Brüder und EU-nuchen
Then they jeer from the sidelines while the United States does the hard and dirty business of keeping the world safe for Europeans. Americans, by contrast, are strong, principled defenders of freedom, standing tall in the patriotic service of the world's last truly sovereign nation-state.	Und dann johlen sie von den Zuschauerrängen, während die USA das schwierige und schmutzige Geschäft erledigen, in der Welt für Sicherheit zu sorgen – auch für die Europäer. Die Amerikaner dagegen sind starke, prinzipiengeleitete Verteidiger der Freiheit, aufrecht im Dienst für das Vaterland, den letzten wahrhaft souveränen Nationalstaat der Welt.
A study should be written on the sexual imagery of these stereotypes. If anti-American Europeans see "the Americans" as bullying cowboys, anti-European Americans see "the Europeans" as limp-wristed pansies. The American is a virile, heterosexual male; the European is female, impotent, or castrated. Militarily, Europeans can't get it up. (The word "eunuchs" is, I discovered, used in the form "EU-nuchs.")	Die sexuelle Konnotation dieser Stereotypen wäre eine Untersuchung wert. Sehen antiamerikanische Europäer „die Amerikaner" als tyrannische Cowboys, so sehen antieuropäische Amerikaner „die Europäer" als warme Brüder. Der Amerikaner ist ein viriles, heterosexuelles Mannsbild, der Europäer ist weiblich, impotent oder kastriert. Vor allem militärisch kriegen die Europäer keinen hoch. Das Wort „Eunuchen" findet auch in der Form „EU-nuchen" Verwendung.
Anti-Europeanism is not symmetrical with anti-Americanism. The emotional leitmotifs of anti-Americanism are resentment mingled with envy; those of anti-Europeanism are irritation mixed with contempt.	Der Antieuropäismus bildet keine Parallele zum Antiamerikanismus. Das Leitmotiv des Antiamerikanismus ist mit Neid durchsetzter Groll; die des Antieuropäismus mit Verachtung durchsetzte Gereiztheit.

by Timothy Garton Ash, in: *Die Zeit*, 28.1.2003 (translated by Karin Wördemann) and the *New York Review of Books*, February 13, 2003

Summit G8, p. 89

3 Living in Europe – A Question of Identity?

We have become so used to the idea of a united Europe that we hardly think about what it really means to us any more. The two girls in the picture have tried to express their views of a European identity in a poster.

Vocabulary training

a. Look up the opposites of the adjectives on the poster and the appropriate noun in a dictionary. Then fill in the grid below.

adjective	opposite	noun
tolerant		
sociable		
straightforward		
understanding		
human		
fair		
respectful		
balanced		
outspoken		
cooperative		

b. Use the adjectives in the grid to create slogans for a campaign on European identity.

Focus on Facts: The European Union

4 Summit G8, p. 93

Mediation

We all know that different nations have different cultural concepts and mentalities. Sociologists worked out the main differences between the so-called 'new world' and the 'old world'.

a Have a look at the following key-words that *are said* to define the American and European mentalities. Choose five terms, take notes in your exercise-books, and then mediate them considering the differing historical, social and cultural backgrounds. → Students' Book, Method Kit, p. 258

America	Europe
Unschuld	Erfahrung
Materialismus	Kultur
Erfolgsstreben	Sicherheitsstreben
Gleichheitsdenken	Klassenbewusstsein
Zukunftsoptimismus	Traditionsbewusstsein
Mobilität	Verwurzelung
Identitäts- und Wurzellosigkeit	Erstarrung im Überkommenen
Jugendkult	Altersverehrung
Freiheitsstreben	Autoritätsgläubigkeit
Puritanismus	Lebensgenuss
Aggressivität gegenüber der Natur	Streben nach Harmonie zwischen Natur und Kultur
Kreativität	Bildungsbürgertum
offene Gesellschaft	geschlossene Gesellschaft

b. Discuss whether you have a more European or American attitude.

Distinctly Canadian – I Wonder What They Are

Summit G8, p. 96

1 Friends in Need

Present participles

A girl from England who has received one of Miss Lumley's packages writes the following letter to the narrator's school in Canada. Rewrite this letter using as many present participle constructions as possible.

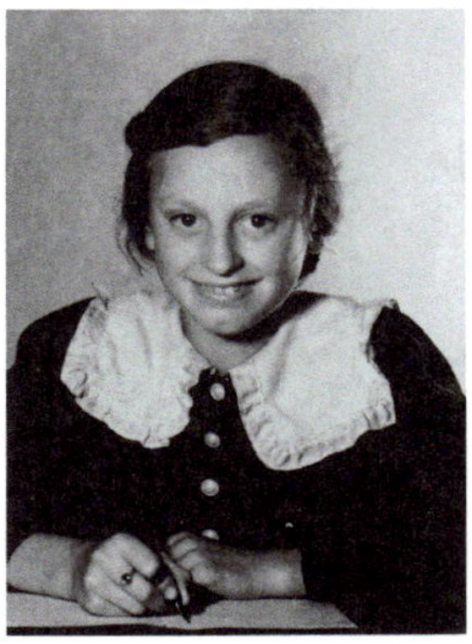

Dear boys and girls in Canada,

Thank you very much for the nice parcel my teacher gave me yesterday. I went home and pushed my bike uphill because the parcel was so heavy! My mum was at work when I got home and so we didn't open the parcel until late in the evening. While I was sitting at the kitchen table and doing my homework, I couldn't concentrate because I desperately wanted to know what was in the parcel. It lay on the sofa and it looked really tempting but I had made up my mind to wait for mum and open it with her. Dad is serving as a soldier somewhere in France and so it is only the two of us at the moment. Mum often lies in bed and cries but I was sure she wouldn't cry this night. I knew she would be happy because of all the things you had sent us. We are lucky because we still live in our home. Many houses have been bombed during the Blitz. These people have lost everything and they have to stay with relatives or even with people they don't know at all.

Mum felt very hungry and tired when she came home from work and so we sat down to dinner immediately. But then we knelt in front of the sofa and cut through the strings of the parcel. What lovely things you've got in Canada! The corduroy trousers are a little too big but I can wear them if I use a belt. As dad is not at home at the moment, we will give the beautiful shirt to granddad. It felt like Christmas and I was lying in bed and dreaming of a shop full of corduroy trousers and Viyella shirts! Thanks very much again. People in Canada are very nice and very generous. Our teacher says you're helping us because we are all part of the British Empire and we must stick together especially in times of hardship and war. When the war is over I'll visit your wonderful country. I'm looking forward to this.

Best wishes,
Sarah Brown from England

Focus on Facts: Canada

2 Summit G8, p. 99

Study the table on eligibility requirements for immigrants who want to settle in Canada, the United States, Australia or the United Kingdom.

Translating terms

a. Translate the following terms into German. Use a dictionary.
→ Students' Book, Method Kit, p. 258

eligibility requirements: ______________________________

dual citizenship: ______________________________

naturalized citizen: ______________________________

eligible immigrant: ______________________________

permanent residence: ______________________________

Eligibility requirements vary from country to country

	Canada	United States	Australia	United Kingdom
Residency requirement	3 of the 4 years prior to application	5 years of continuous residence (i. e. no more than one year absent, resided in one state for at least 3 months)	2 years of permanent residence	5 years of residence, with the last year being continuous
Language requirement	Knowledge of basic English or French	Ability to read, write, speak and understand ordinary English	Understanding of basic English	Sufficient knowledge of English, Welsh of Scottish Gaelic
Knowledge requirement	Basic knowledge of Canada – geography, history, government	Knowledge and understanding of U.S. history and government	Knowledge and understanding of the responsibilities and privileges of Australian citizenship	Not applicable
Dual citizenship for naturalized citizens	Yes	No	Yes	Yes
Foreign-born as a percentage of the population	18 %	11 %	22 %	8 %
Percent of naturalized citizens among eligible immigrants	84 %	40 %	75 %	56 %

Data: Citizenship and Immigration Canada, Statistics Canada, U.S. Citizenship and Immigration Services, U.S. Census Bureau, Australian Citizenship Council, Australian Bureau of Statistics, and British Home Office: Immigration and Nationality Directorate.

b. In which country can people most easily become naturalized citizens? Speculate about the reasons.

Analysing a survey

Summit G8, p. 101

3 Maria Campbell – A Métis Author and Political Activist

Idioms **a.** Match the idioms with their explanations and find a good German translation for the idioms.

Idiomatic expression		Meaning
1. to drive sb. up the wall jdn. wahnsinnig machen	1g	**a.** to accept the blame or responsibility alone, even though other people were responsible
2. to jump for joy __________		**b.** sth. happens or sb. says sth. that makes you think very seriously about it
3. to be out of touch with sth. __________		**c.** to say sth. tactless and embarrassing
4. to give sb. food for thought __________		**d.** to be in a very difficult or dangerous situation
5. sth. works like magic __________		**e.** sth. brings you suddenly back to reality
6. to be one's bread and butter __________		**f.** when sb. used to know about sth. but doesn't know the latest developments
7. to put one's foot in it __________		**g.** make sb. very angry
8. to be in dire straits __________		**h.** be very happy and excited about sth. that has happened
9. to carry the can __________		**i.** be an activity you do to get the money you need
10. to come down to earth with a bang __________		**j.** sth. works immediately and very well indeed

b. Put the appropriate idioms into the following sentences.

1. Most white people ____________________ the living conditions of the native and Métis peoples in Canada.

2. For a certain time even prostitution ______________ Maria Campbell's __________ __________ because she did not have any profession and did not know how to earn her living.

3. She __________ really ____________________.

4. Experiences with drugs and alcohol made her ____________________ ______________________________.

5. For a long time she felt as if she had to ____________________. Native peoples were treated like second-class citizens by the whites and Maria thought low of herself and her abilities.

6. The employee in the Welfare Office ____________ Maria ____________ by suggesting she should spend the rest of all her money before asking for help.

7. Only when Maria Campbell met a civil rights worker who told her about the unjust treatment of the native and Métis peoples in Canada it ____________ and caused her to become actively involved in a native organization.

8. When she told her people about her own life and asked them to change their lives too, her words ____________. People started to become courageous and to resist the current laws on Indian Affairs.

9. However, Maria Campbell sometimes ____________ when she was talking to white people. She still had to learn that there were also white people who helped the Canadian indigenous population.

10. Finally, Maria Campbell started to write her autobiography to help her people. She could ____________ because of her late success as a writer and political activist.

Minorities Population in Toronto

4 Summit G8, p. 107

Describing statistics

Describe the following chart. Use the Method Kit in your Students' Book, p. 284.
Is Toronto a Canadian city? Give reasons.

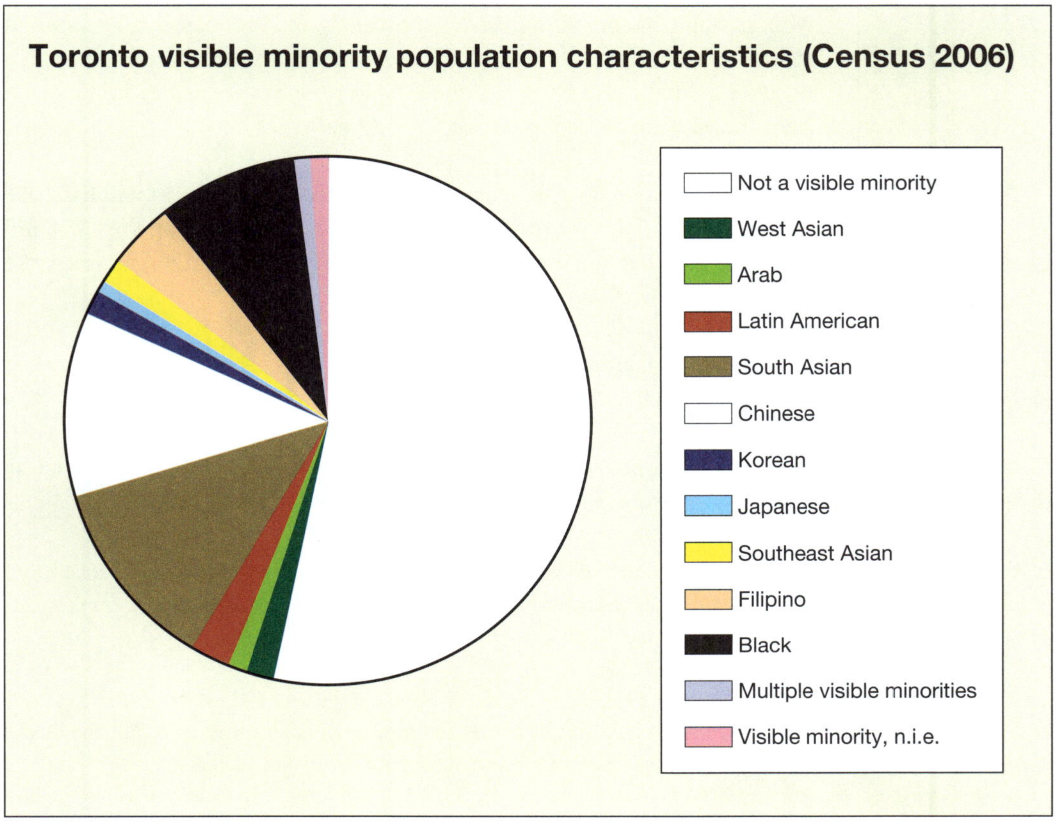

All in Society – I Wonder Who We Are

Summit G8, p. 110

1 Debating Society

Expressing opinions

The following expressions are commonly used when agreeing and disagreeing with someone or admitting that you were wrong. They will come in handy when you hold debates or discussions in class.

I. Agreeing

- I think you're right.
- I agree with you.
- That's right/true.
- I couldn't agree more.
- Exactly!/Absolutely!
- You're dead/absolutely right! *(infml.)*
- My sentiments/feelings exactly.

II. Disagreeing/showing doubt

- (I'm afraid) I disagree with you.
- (Unfortunately) I can't agree with you.
- I take/see your point, but ...
- I agree with you in principle, but ...
- Well, actually (I think) ...
- That's not the way I see it! *(infml.)*
- (Oh) come on! *(infml.)*
- You can't be serious! *(infml.)*

III. Admitting that you were wrong

- Yes, sorry, you're right.
- You might/may/could be right (about that).
- Ok, you do have a point (there).
- Silly me! Of course you're right. *(infml.)*
- Good point! *(infml.)*
- I admit, I was wrong.
- Yes, I didn't take that into account.

a. Use the phrases from the boxes above to write an answer to each case. Then, have mini-debates on the issues.

"Can we ask you to not wear that T-shirt, Bill?"

1. Your teacher tells you about a new health policy measure that your school will be introducing and says: "The school has decided to remove vending machines because they promote unhealthy eating." You disagree.

2. An editorial in a well-known American newspaper claims: "In Germany, with its tragic history of exclusive nationalism and race-based citizenship, it is an intellectual revolution [that] some of Germany's most conservative politicians are finally accepting that there is no reason someone cannot be German and Muslim at the same time." You agree.

3. You tell a friend from England that Germany won the 1954 and the 1966 Football World Cup. Your friend points out that Germany won the 1954 and the 1974 cup but not the 1966 championship. You admit that you were wrong.

4. In a report you read in a youth magazine, a scientist claims that young people should get at least eight hours of sleep a day to support a healthy lifestyle. You strongly agree.

5. An American exchange student at your school explains that the death penalty is an effective way to fight violent crime. You disagree strongly.

6. On returning from a trip to America, you tell your class that teenagers can get a driving licence there at the age of 14. Your teacher tells you that in most states you have to be at least 16 to drive a car. You admit that you were wrong.

b. Think of other scenarios in which people might agree/disagree with each other or admit they were wrong. Write dialogues using the phrases from above and/or debate the issues in class.

What If?

2 Summit G8, p. 117

If-clauses

Look at the cartoon on p. 117 of your Students' Book. Write down what is going on inside the young woman's head. Pay attention to the correct tenses when completing the following sentences.

1. If the governors hadn't decided positively, ______________________________

2. If I keep on wearing my headscarf, ______________________________

3. I will be considered a threat to the British way of life unless ______________________________

4. My family would be disappointed if ______________________________

5. If I hadn't come to this office, ______________________________

6. Being called a threat to civilization is hard to understand unless ______________________________

7. If I stopped living according to my religion, ______________________________

8. Now I can start a career like British women, provided ______________________________

9. If I still lived in Pakistan, ______________________________

Focus on Facts: Multiculturalism

3 Summit G8, p. 118

Active and passive voice

a. Look at the following sentences related to your Students' Book, pp. 118 f. and transform them from passive into active voice or vice versa. Remember that you might have to find suitable subjects or *by*-agents for some phrases.

Example: In the 1940s and 1950s, many immigrants came to Britain from countries which **are known** as the Commonwealth.

... countries which **people know** as the Commonwealth.

1. People **saw** themselves as guest workers.

2. An immigration permit **is** also **granted** to those immigrants whose grand-parents or parents were British.

3. Work permits **are assigned** to skilled immigrants who have skills or exceptional abilities that contribute to the British economy.

4. It also implies that each group of immigrants **assimilates into** American society at its own pace.

5. The ideas of cultural pluralism and multiculturalism **have** largely **replaced** the idea of assimilation.

6. Alternative models where immigrants retain their native cultures such as the 'salad bowl' or the 'symphony' **are** more often **used** by prominent sociologists to describe how cultures and ethnicities mix in the United States.

b. Transform the speech bubble in the cartoon into passive voice.

Summit G8, p. 127, 131

4 Jodi Picoult: Nineteen Minutes

The following texts are taken from the beginning of the latest novel by the bestseller author Jodi Picoult, who develops the story of a 17-year-old boy walking into his school with guns instead of books and killing ten people there. Later, he will excuse his shooting with bullying he was not able to bear.

C-test

a. Fill in the gaps with the appropriate endings. The number of missing letters is given.

Jodi Picoult

In nineteen minutes, you can mow the front lawn, color your hair, watch a third of a hockey game. In nine____ minutes, y__ can ba__ scones o_ get a to___ filled b_ a dentist; y__ can fo__ laundry f__ a family o_ five.

Nine____ minutes i_ how lo__ it ta___ the Tenn_____ Titans t_ sell o__ of tic____ to t__ play-offs. It__ the len___ of a sit___, minus t__ commercials. It__ the dri____ distance fr__ the Ver____ border t_ the to__ of Ster____, New Hamp_____.

In nine____ minutes, y__ can st__ the wo___, or y__ can ju__ jump o__ it. I_ nineteen min____, you c__ get rev____.

from *Nineteen Minutes* by Jodi Picoult. London, Hodder & Stoughton, 2008, p. 5

Vocabulary training

b. Complete the text with the words given below. Then, translate this special vocabulary.

superior court judge	guilty	courtroom	legal system
appointment	district court judge	prosecutors	

Alex had been a ____________________ **(1)** now for thirty-four days. She'd believed that, having proved her mettle[1] as a ____ **(2)** for the past five years, this time around the ____________________ **(3)** might be easier. But at forty, she was still the youngest judge in the state. She still had to fight to establish herself as a fair justice – her history as a public defender preceded her into her ______________ **(4)**, and ______________________ **(5)** assumed she'd side with the defense. When Alex had submitted her name years ago for the bench[2], it had been with the sincere desire to make sure people in this ___________________________ **(6)** were innocent until proven _________ **(7)**. She just never anticipated that, as a judge, she might not be given the same benefit of that doubt.

from *Nineteen Minutes* by Jodi Picoult. London, Hodder & Stoughton, 2008, pp. 5–6

[1]**mettle** courage and determination – [2]**bench** the position of being a judge in a court of law

c. Work out a word map with all the words and phrases around the topic "Crime and punishment" that you can think of. Also use the vocabulary given in your Students' Book, pp. 130 and 133. You may start like this:

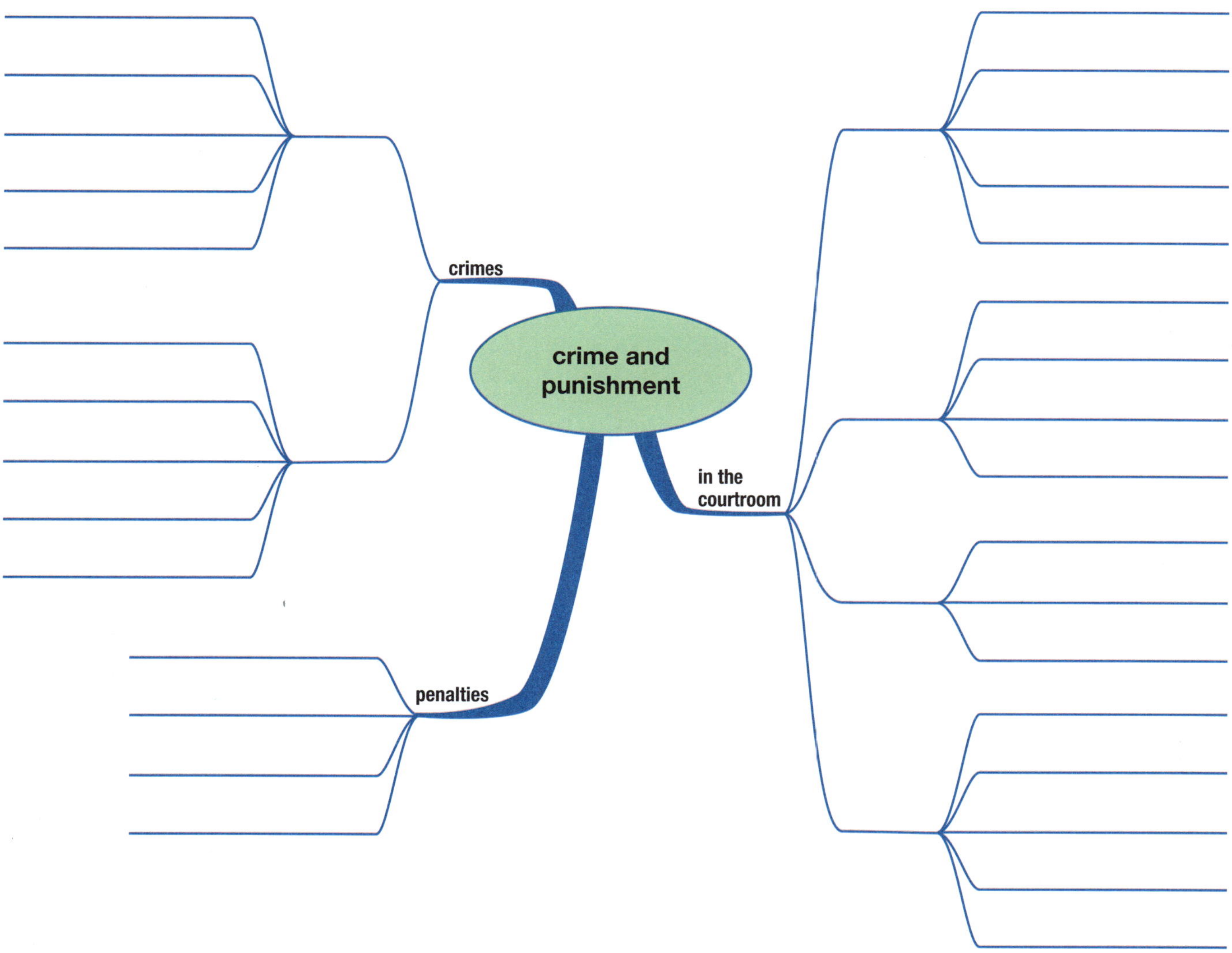

Summit G8, p. 133

5 Would You Like To Be a Chav?

Vocabulary training

The following gapped text describes *chavs*, a new sub-culture in Britain. Fill in the gaps with the right forms of the 12 words given below:

adult	low-paid	to apply	ASBOs	casual	to commit
criticism	critics	to label	glamour	to feature	to embody

Chav is a derogatory term which is ________________ (1) to a certain group of people in the United Kingdom. The stereotypical image of a chav is a white aggressive teen or young ________________ (2), of working class background, wearing branded sports and ________________ (3) clothing, e.g. baseball caps, being unemployed or in a ____________ (4) job, fighting and ________________ (5) petty crimes.

The chav culture has been portrayed extensively in British media. The Welsh rap group, Goldie Lookin' Chain, have been described as both ________________ (6) and satirising the chav aesthetic. Footballer Wayne Rooney and his wife Coleen, rapper Lady Sovereign, ________________ (7) model Jordan, and former Big Brother contestant Jade Goody have also been ________________ (8) "chavs" by British tabloids. The famous sketch comedy series Little Britain ________________ (9) a character with some similarities, Vicky Pollard.

The widespread use of the chav stereotype, however, has come under ________________ (10). Some argue that serious social problems such as Anti-Social Behaviour Orders (________________) (11), teenage pregnancy, delinquency and alcoholism in low-income areas should not be mocked at. ________________ (12) of the term have also argued that its proponents are neo-snobs, and that its increasing popularity raises questions about how British society deals with social mobility and class.

Summit G8, p. 141

6 Focus on Facts: Social Welfare in the USA

Vocabulary training

How much money does a single, childless and unemployed 40-year-old man get in Denmark, France, Germany and the United States?

a. Translate the underlined words in the first two texts. Then fill in the gaps in the remaining two texts.

❶ Denmark

How much: 90 percent of gross wages Bruttolöhne to a ceiling ________________ (1) of $ 1,994 a month. It is all taxable ________________ (2).

For how long: Four years

Obligations: Must participate in labour training ________________ (3) or other job re-integration programs ________________ (4).

Who is eligible ________________ (5): Workers who were employed for 52 weeks during the preceding three years and paid into the voluntary plan ________________ (6) – as 90 percent do – for one year.

France ❷

How much: 57.4 percent of gross salary ______________ (7), to a maximum payment of $ 7,015 a month. But payments are taxed, especially at high income levels ______________ (8).

For how long: Up to 23 months, depending on employment history ______________ (9).

Obligations: France has had mixed ______________ (10) success with the plan to tie benefits ______________ (11) to searching for a new job.

Who is eligible: Under the mandatory plan ______________ (12), workers with six months of employment within the preceding 22 months ______________ (13).

Germany ❸

How much: 60 percent of net wages to a ______________ (14) of $ 2,018 per month.

For how long: 12 months

Obligations: Germany has expanded its ______________ (15) programs and cut ______________ (16) that kick in once the unemployment insurance ______________ (17) out.

Who is ______________ (18): Those with a previous ______________ (19) of up to $ 74,880 in western Germany and $ 63,360 in eastern Germany who have been employed for at least 12 months within the ______________ (20) three years. The plan is ______________ (21).

The United States ❹
(Pennsylvania and Lousisana)

How much: States ______________ (22), but up to $ 486 a week in Pennsylvania, and $ 258 in Louisiana. Federal tax applies.

For ______________ (23): 16 to 26 weeks in Pennsylvania, 21 to 26 in Louisiana, unless Washington makes extended benefits available in special ______________ (24).

______________ (25): Must be able and ______________ (26) to work. Louisiana requires acceptance of jobs paying 60 percent of previous ______________ (27).

Who is eligible: Workers who earned a minimum ______________ (28) in a one-year base period ($ 1,320 in Pennsylvania and $ 1,200 in Louisiana).

b. Compare the situation of the 40-year-old childless, single and un-employed man in the different countries by means of a grid.

→ Students' Book, Method Kit, p. 264

Summit G8, p. 142

7 Guilty Parents?

Parents who have made uncommon choices in bringing up their children might feel guilty. Asked if this was the case, they came up with the following answers.

Reported speech

Put their statements into indirect speech.

Judey: You ask me if I feel guilty. The only thing that would make me reassess what I'm doing would be if Harvey wasn't happy, or seeing something going on in the nursery that I didn't like.

Judey reflected ...

Alexa: The study doesn't make me think again about anything I've done. Beth is very bright, very interactive, very helpful. In this day and age parents like me have to depend on childcare.

Alexa pointed out ...

Simon: Guilty? Me? It's irksome that there's been no mention of fathers. I'm confused: is it that a child will be better off with a parent, whether it's a mother or a father? In which case I agree. Or will a mother be better than a father – in which case I couldn't agree.

Simon wanted to know ...

Karina and Richard: You suggest that we should feel guilty. This sort of study makes you feel uneasy about things that you have no choice over. For us nursery care is one of life's musts. We don't have the luxury of living on one wage.

Karina and Richard accused their interviewer of ...

Joanna Moorhead, Lucy Ward: "If Not Nursery, What?" from *The Guardian*, October 8, 2005, pp. 4–5

Summit G8, p. 145

8 Focus on Facts: Social Classes

Matching

Social class assumes three simplified categories: lower, middle and upper class. Match the words given below with the class they characterize the most in British society.

blue-collar worker | common accent | conformist life | council flat | exclusivity | family background | fish and chips | GCSE | welfare | landowner | Oxbridge | political privileges | 'Us' | posh accent | public school | regional accent | respectability | 'salatariat' | self-employed | semi-detached house | stately home | 'Them' | suits and bowler hats | terraced house | title | university degree | trade-union member | white-collar employee | vote Labour Party

lower class	middle class	upper class

Trying to Do it All

9 Summit G8, p. 169

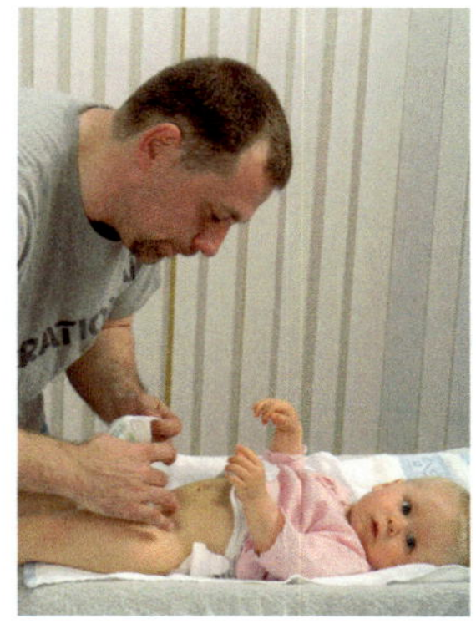

Women aren't the only ones having a rough go in Europe. Men, these days, are embracing fatherhood with the round-the-clock involvement their partners have always dreamed of – changing diapers, handling night feedings, packing lunches and bandaging knees. The time British dads spend with their kids has risen eightfold over the last 30 years. Today, 79 percent say they'd be happy to stay at home and 9 out of 10 say they're as confident as their partners in looking after the kids. "These dads are going to be a guide and a mentor in a much more visible way than their own fathers were," says Armin A. Brott, author of *Fathering Your Toddler*.

That's good news for Europe, whose economic future depends on a rising birth rate. Studies show that women with involved partners are more inclined to have more than one child. To tempt moms back to work, governments are also putting in place more policies to help dads take time off. Britain, for instance, announced recently that fathers would be entitled to up to six months of paternity leave. In Germany, companies are required by law to give all employees up to three-years parental leave and guarantee their jobs on return. But all these devoted dads may have a harder time with the same issues women have faced for decades: namely, how to balance work and family. "There's a constant feeling of guilt," says Robin Mungrah, a 37-year-old London accountant with two children. "No matter how early I leave work or how often I take the kids to Legoland on the weekends, it never seems enough." Unlike women, many find they're negotiating their new roles with little support or information. "Men in my generation [25–40] have a fear of becoming dads because we have no role models," says Jon Smith, author of *The Bloke's Guide to Pregnancy*. They often find themselves excluded from mothers' support networks, and are eyed warily on the playground.

from *Newsweek*, February 27, 2006 [slightly modified]

a. Explain the underlined words.

Reading comprehension

b. Tick the correct answers:

1. The new generation of fathers is

- a aging.
- b sad.
- c funny.
- d a help for their partners.

2. Women

- a are better off today than in the past.
- b are worse off today than in the past.
- c are in the same situation as in the past.
- d are enjoying their partners being devoted fathers.

3. Armin A. Brott

- a is a toddler.
- b is an author.
- c is a guide.
- d is a mentor.

4. Great Britain and Germany

- a have adopted the same policy to lure women back to work.
- b allow both partners time off for raising their children.
- c fire all parents.
- d handle the situation differently.

5. Robin Mungrah

- a is guilty.
- b feels guilty.
- c makes his partner feel guilty.
- d doesn't have any feelings of guilt.

6. Male role models

- a are hard to find.
- b are easy to find.
- c are not defined.
- d are confined.

Going Global

1 How to Deal with Undocumented Workers in the U.S.?

Summit G8, p. 152

Working with cartoons

Cartoons are usually humorous illustrations and often deal with important people or topics in a critical way. Take a look at the following cartoon and its position on illegal immigrants.

a. Description: Describe the cartoon and name its theme.

b. Analysis: Point out how the figures are presented, and explain what point the cartoonist is trying to make.

c. Evaluation: Explain the effect the cartoon has on you and state why you (do not) like it.
→ Students' Book, Method Kit, p. 285

2 Temporary Worker Program

Summit G8, p. 152

With the numbers of illegal workers in the U.S. soaring, officials see the need to take action, e.g. with a temporary worker program.

Vocabulary training

Read the text and fill in the gaps with the correct forms of the words given.

aliens	business	credit	employment	foreign
incentives	job offer	legal	native	permanently
portion	reasonable	simply	temporary worker program	
to be eligible	to enforce	to expire	to return	tough
undocumented				

I [the then U.S. President G.W. Bush] propose a new temporary worker program that will match willing __________ (1) workers with willing American employers, when no Americans can be found to fill the jobs. This program will offer __________ (2) status, as temporary workers, to the millions of __________ (3) men and women now employed in the United States, and to those in foreign countries who seek to participate in the program and have been offered __________ (4) here. This new system should be clear and efficient, so employers are able to find workers quickly and __________ (5).
All who participate in the __________ (6) must have a job, or, if not living in the United States, a __________ (7). The legal status granted by this program will last three years and will be renewable — but it will have an end. Participants who do not remain employed, who do not follow the rules of the program, or who break the law will not __________ (8) for continued participation and will be required to __________ (9) to their home.
Under my proposal, employers have key responsibilities. Employers who extend job offers must first make every __________ (10) effort to find an American worker for the job at hand. Our government will develop a quick and simple system for employers to search for American workers. Employers must not hire undocumented __________ (11) or temporary workers whose legal status has __________ (12). They must report to the government the temporary workers they hire, and who leave their employment, so that we can keep track of people in the program, and better __________ (13) immigration laws. There must be strong workplace enforcement with __________ (14) penalties for anyone, for any employer violating these laws. [...]
This program expects temporary workers to return __________ (15) to their home countries after their period of work in the United States has expired. And there should be financial __________ (16) for them to do so. I will work with foreign governments on a plan to give temporary workers __________ (17), when they enter their own nation's retirement system, for the time they have worked in America. I also support making it easier for temporary workers to contribute a __________ (18) of their earnings to tax-preferred savings accounts, money they can collect as they return to their __________ (19) countries. After all, in many of those countries, a small nest egg is what is necessary to start their own __________ (20), or buy some land for their family.

from www.whitehouse.gov/news/releases/2004/01/20040107-3.html [07.01.2004]

Summit G8, p. 156

3 Focus on Facts: Economy

a. The *Focus on Facts* page on economy lists several reasons that explain the power of the U.S. economy. Read the passage in your Students' Book, and then complete the mind map with your book closed.

b. The following table shows economic terms on the left and a jumbled list of definitions on the right. Find the pairs and write the matching numbers and letters in the middle column.

1. privatization	1 p	**a.** The use of machines to do work that was previously done by people
2. nationalization		**b.** Generic term for tertiary and quaternary sectors
3. productivity		**c.** This sector involves the provision of services to businesses as well as final consumers.
4. primary sector		**d.** Not for the whole day or week in which people work
5. secondary sector		**e.** All the people who work for a particular company or organization
6. service sector		**f.** Sector where natural resources are changed into primary products
7. tertiary sector		**g.** The rate at which a worker, a company or a country produces goods, and the amount produced, compared with how much time, work and money is needed to produce them
8. quaternary sector		**h.** Sector where a finished, usable product is created or a product processed
9. part-time		**i.** This sector is about gaining, processing and sharing information.
10. workforce		**j.** To put an industry or a company under the control of the government, which then becomes its owner
11. balance of payments		**k.** Industry that uses large machinery to produce metal, coal, vehicles, etc.
12. automation		**l.** Specialization of cooperative labour into specific clearly-defined tasks and roles
13. division of labour		**m.** The difference between the amount a country pays for imports and the amount it receives for exports in a particular period of time
14. salary		**n.** A regular amount of money that you earn, usually every week, for work or services
15. heavy industry		**o.** Money that people working in an office get paid every month
16. wage		**p.** Selling a business or an industry so that it is no longer owned by the government

Subordinate clauses

c. Rewrite the parts of the sentences in bold type by using either a participle construction, a relative clause or an adverbial clause instead.

1. **Having reduced** their hours, more and more workers see their chances of promotion passing by, a report from the Equal Opportunities Commission (EOC) indicates.

2. **As their bosses don't take them seriously anymore**, more than 5.5 million of Great Britain's 7 million part-time workers are stuck in jobs for which they are overqualified.

3. **Lacking the confidence or the knowledge to introduce flexible or part-time working,** managers are to blame, the EOC report states.

4. According to the report **published** last month, there's a slowly growing number of employers **moving away from 'presenteeism'**.

5. **Realizing the advantages for business and staff morale,** these employers encourage flexible working arrangements.

Women's Work

4 Summit G8, p. 158

In most developed countries, women make up less than half of the workforce. But the nature – and rewards – of their work vary between countries.

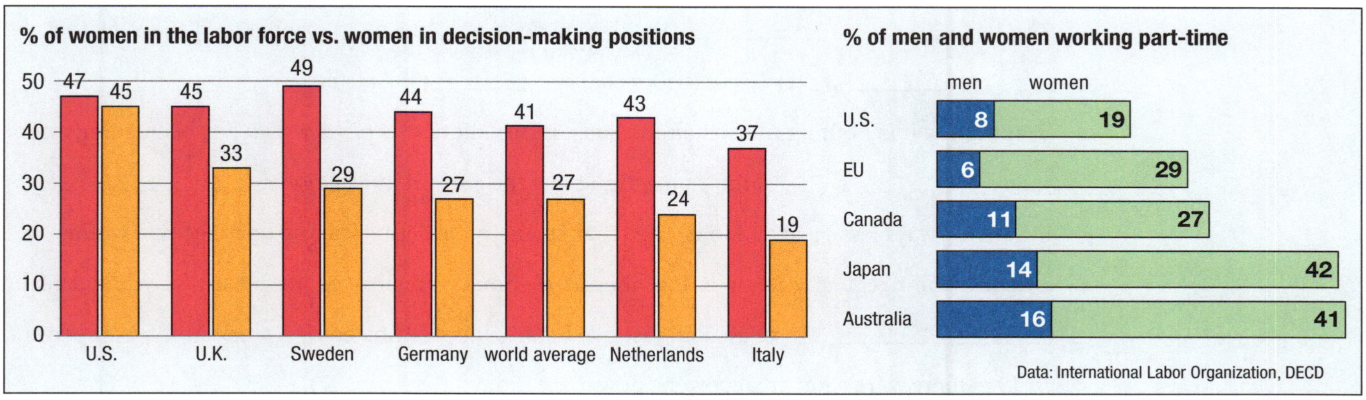

a. Analyse the diagram and comment on the results. See → Students' Book, Method Kit, p. 284 to find some helpful expressions.

Working with statistics

b. Fill in the gaps in the following text with the appropriate words and endings.

C-test

The Myth of Women's Equality in Europe

For all the myths of equality that Europe tells itself, the Continent is by and large a woeful place for a woman who aspires to lead. According t_ a pa___ published b_ the Intern_______ Labor Organi______, women acc____ for 45 per____ of high-le___ decision mak___ in Ame____, including legis______, senior offi_____ and mana____ across all ty___ of busi____. In t__ UK, wo___ hold 33 per____ of th___ jobs. In Swe___ they ho__ 29 percent. Ger____ comes i_ at ju__ under 27 per____ and Ita____ women ho__ a pathetic 19 per____ of po___ jobs.

It i_ not th__ European wo___ are st___ in t__ house. Af___ all, wo___ make u_ 57 percent o_ the EU 15's work_____. The re__ problem i_ that Eur___ has be__ consistently una___ to t__ the hig____ potential o_ its fem___ workers, w__ represent ha__ of t__ college grad_____ in mo__ countries.

Wo___, it se___, can ha__ a job – b__ not a hi__-powered car___.

c. Summarize the article in one German sentence.
→ Students' Book, Method Kit, p. 258

Mediating

Summit G8, p. 166

5 Focus on Facts: Globalisation

Vocabulary training

The following article gives a definition of the phenomenon of globalisation. Complete the text by filling in the following words and phrases in the correct order.

G8	developing	degree	kind	raw
telecommunications		economy	phenomenon	products
world trade	monetary	new	financial	globalisation
developing	centuries	new	changes	global
Internet				

The term ____________________ **(1)** is a modern one, but many people hold the view that the ____________________ **(2)** it describes is not __________ **(3)** at all.

Sceptics say it is nothing more than the latest incarnation[1] of a process that has been going on for many ________________ **(4)**; some argue that the current international ________________ **(5)** is in many ways less open and integrated than it was in the period leading up to the first world war.

Another point regularly made is that the international economy of the present day is not really ________________ **(6)** at all and, just like before, it is dominated by a small number of players.

In 1914 there were eight great powers, now there is the __________ **(7)**.

As Paul Hirst, Professor of Social Theory at Birkbeck College, University of London, points out, the difference now is that now the Russians have turned up as poor guests and Austro-Hungary has been replaced by Canada.

The opposite view – that globalisation is indeed a ____________ **(8)** phenomenon – has been articulated by many writers, many of whose works have become required reading for protesters and advocates alike, such as Naomi Klein and Noreena Hertz, to name but two. They believe that the developments of the past few decades have spurred ________________ **(9)** so large that the world has indeed entered a qualitatively new (and unwelcome) era.

The statistics are certainly convincing: since 1950, the volume of ________________ **(10)** has increased by 20 times. And from just 1997 to 1999, flows of foreign investment nearly doubled, from $ 468bn to $ 827bn.

Thomas Friedman, a New York Times columnist and author of another oft-cited book on globalisation, *The Lexus and the Olive Tree*, argues that today's era of globalisation is different both in ______________ **(11)** and in______________ **(12)** from previous eras.

He says while the previous era of globalisation was built around falling transport costs, today's globalisation is built around falling ____________________ **(13)** costs, which are able to weave[2] the world together even tighter.

[1] **incarnation** manifestation – [2] **to weave** here: to unite different aspects

These technologies mean that ________________ (14) countries don't just have to trade their ____________ (15) materials to the West and get finished ______________ (16) in return; now, ______________ (17) countries can become big producers as well.

Using an example of his mother's use of new technology to show how the world has changed, he asks rhetorically: "Was your great grandmother playing bridge with Frenchmen on the ______________ (18) in 1900?"

One area where many, but certainly not all, experts tend to be in agreement about the novelty of globalisation is the ________________ (19) and ________________ (20) arena.

Lewis Williamson: "Globalisation: World-changing or word-changing?" from *The Guardian*, October 31, 2002

The Evolution of Man

6 Summit G8, p. 166

Working with visuals

a. Describe the cartoons using words from the lists given.

b. Find a caption for every cartoon.

c. Compare the cartoons according to their similarities and differences, and sum up their gist in one sentence. → Students' Book, Method Kit, p. 285

d. Draw your own cartoon about the evolution of man including a caption or title.

❶

process of evolution,
crown of creation, club

2

to descend from, cavemen, Vikings, civilized English gentleman, bowler hat, facial expression, to keep a stiff upper lip

3

endpoint of evolution, security checks, metal detectors, amphibians

4

Summit G8, p. 166

7 Creating Collocations

Collocations are combinations of different words that frequently go together, often a noun and a verb.

Vocabulary training

a. Find the collocations.

1. to hold	**a.** a disease
2. to keep	**b.** methods
3. to encounter	**c.** a problem
4. to spark	**d.** a fact
5. to raise	**e.** an opinion
6. to carry out	**f.** hopes
7. to acknowledge	**g.** a debate
8. to tackle	**h.** difficulties
9. to apply	**i.** a treatment
10. to cure	**j.** a promise
11. to come down with	**k.** an anaesthetic
12. to undergo	**l.** antibiotics
13. to be given	**m.** research
14. to be on	**n.** an infection

Translation

b. Translate the following sentences into English using the collocations from above.
→ Students' Book, Method Kit, p. 258

1. Wissenschaftler treffen oft auf Schwierigkeiten, wenn sie bei Forschungen Methoden anwenden, die von der Gesellschaft als ethisch nicht tragbar betrachtet werden.

2. Auf dem Gebiet der Gentechnologie geschieht es leider häufig, dass in Patienten Hoffnungen geweckt werden, die später nicht erfüllt werden.

3. Kranke, die Antibiotika einnehmen, bekommen oft zusätzlich noch eine Infektion.

4. Um Krankheiten erfolgreich heilen zu können, müssen wissenschaftliche Untersuchungen durchgeführt werden.

5. Bevor Patienten eine Behandlung bekommen, müssen sie sorgfältig untersucht werden.

6. Wissenschaftler vertreten oft die Meinung, dass eine Vollnarkose nur in Ausnahmefällen gegeben werden sollte.

Disposing of Household Appliances

8 Summit G8, p. 170

These days electronic household appliances break down very easily and have to be disposed of appropriately for environmental reasons. The following manual helps you recycle them properly. However, it has been very badly translated into English by a non-native speaker, who tried to generate a very formal English text. For that reason, it is even more difficult to understand.

Prepositions

a. He also had problems with prepositions. Help him choose the correct one.

Disposal from/of/on Old Electrical & Electronic Equipment (Applicable from/in/at the European Union and other European countries with separate collection systems)

This symbol from/of/on the product or from/of/on its packaging indicates that this product shall not be treated as household waste. Instead it shall be handed on to/over to/in the applicable collection point for/in order to/until the recycling of electrical and electronic equipment. By/because of/with ensuring this product is disposed about/of/on correctly, you will help prevent potential negative consequences in/on/for the environment and human health, which could otherwise be caused by/through/in inappropriate waste handling from/on/of this product. The recycling of materials will help to/in/by conserve natural resources. In order to/For/Instead of more detailed information over/in/about recycling to/of/by this product, please contact your local city office, your household waste disposal service or the shop where you purchased the product.

b. Write your own, less complicated version of the manual.

Summit G8, p. 172

9 Cause and Effect

Working with cartoons

Cartoons are usually humorous illustrations and often deal with important people or topics in a critical way. Take a look at how the following cartoon portrays the problem of obesity.

→ Students' Book, Method Kit, p. 285

a. Description: Name the theme of the cartoon and describe the details of the chain reaction depicted above.

Error spotting

b. Cross out the wrong forms of the analysis of the cartoon.

- **Caption and text**
  - Obvious/obviously, the clear/clearly yet blunt/bluntly and simplistic/simplistically caption claims that obese people are to blame for everything bad in/on the world.
  - The extensive use of "scientific words" and language is meant to give the impression of/for objectivity and clarity.

- **Topical relevance**
  - Obesity is widely seen as a mayor/major threat to/for first world economys/economies and health systems.
- **Humorous effect is created through:**
  - the juxtaposition of the seeming/seemingly "objective" and "scientific" to/with the truly/true trivial, e. g. the overexaggeration of/in the "scientific" claim made in the caption,
  - the unimportant/inimportant and ludicrous factors included in the "scientific" flowchart (popping button, tipping box, etc.),
  - the dramatic extent of the problem/the problem's dramatic extent,
  - the simplistic causal modell/model,
  - the use of clichés, e. g./f. ex. the cream cake, the ridiculous labels, or
  - the evil spy with dark sunglasses.
- **The cartoonist's attitude and intention**
  - The cartoon includes all the topical problems and nightmares who/that humanity faces in one cartoon and links them in/to one trite model.
  - Hyperbole is used to trivialize the matter: Although the matters addressed are definitely relevant to/for the world, the method of presenting them trivializes them.
  - All that possibly reveals that the cartoonist is fed up with/about hearing all the buzz words repeated by/from the doomsday prophets.

Focus on Facts: Global Warming

10 Summit G8, p. 172

Vocabulary training

a. Fill in the missing words.

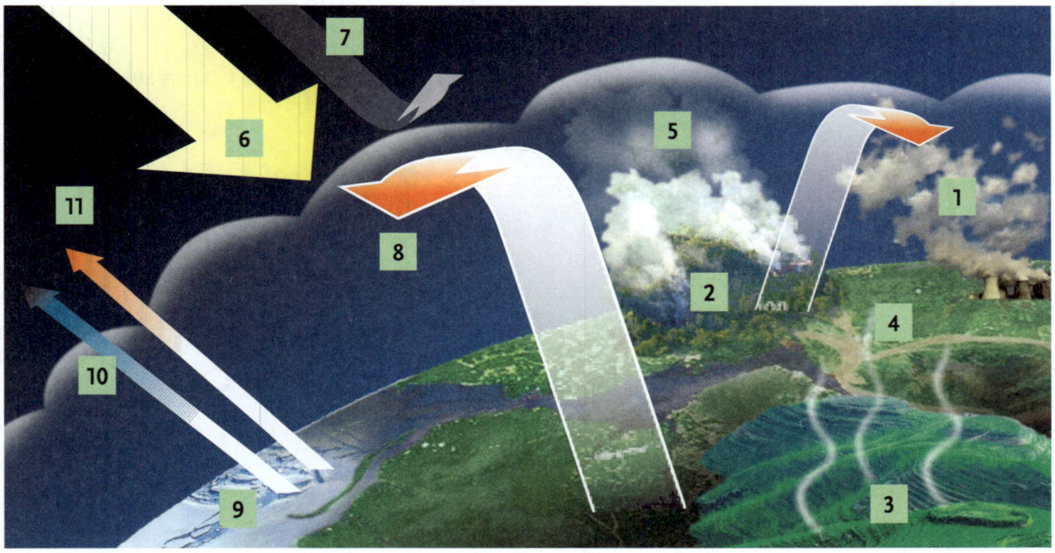

1 ______	5 ______	9 ______
2 ______	6 ______	10 ______
3 ______	7 ______	11 ______
4 ______	8 ______	→ ______

Working with cartoons

b. Take a look at the cartoon below. In the box next to it, replace everything you can see with words. Use nouns, verbs and adjectives. Then describe the cartoon to your partner. What is the message of the cartoon? → Students' Book, Method Kit, p. 285

EARTH

COW

Grammar

c. The following text is about consequences of climate change. Fill in the gaps using the correct forms of the verbs given.

Long Range Weather Forecast: Hot, Dry and French

Southern England ______________ **(to have/1)** the climate of the Champagne region of France in 25 years' time, the Environment Secretary said yesterday.

______________ **(to launch/2)** his department's review of the effects of climate change on the UK, he ______________ **(to say/3)** the climate ______________ **(to already change/4)** noticeably and ______________ **(to continue/5)** to do so until the "familiar landscape of Suffolk ______________ **(to grow/6)** sunflowers and maize."

After another 25 years, the climate ______________ **(to shift/7)** again, with southern England ______________ **(to resemble/8)** the Bordeaux region then and the Champagne climate ______________ **(to move/9)** to Yorkshire.

Rain and windstorms, however, ______________ **(to become/10)** more frequent.

Paul Brown, in: *The Guardian*, July 3, 1996

Game Boys? Child Soldiers!

11 Summit G8, p. 175

Mediating

a. Take a look at the advertisements and translate them into English.
→ Students' Book, Method Kit, p. 258

Focus on Facts: Supranational and International Institutions

12 Summit G8, p. 179

Quiz

a. After having studied the *Focus on Facts* page in your Students' Book carefully, test your knowledge. One answer is correct.

Question no. 1: When was the United Nations founded?	
a. 1776	**b.** 1865
c. 1952	**d.** 1945
Question no. 2: What is not an aim of the UN?	
a. human rights issues	**b.** spread of non-governmental organizations
c. cooperation in international law	**d.** economic development
Question no. 3: What does CSO mean?	
a. Citizens' Problem-Solving Organization	**b.** Children's Service Only
c. Change Solidarity Order	**d.** Civil Society Organization
Question no. 4: Which one is a supranational governmental organization?	
a. SOS Kinderdörfer	**b.** Open Society Institute
c. United Nations Children's Fund	**d.** Amnesty International

Question no. 5: What does 'amnesty' (as in "Amnesty International") mean?	
a. official order by a government to release prisoners	**b.** ancient document that requires the right to trial
c. Latin word for "freedom"	**d.** Sioux word for "loss of memory"
Question no. 6: What does "Médecins sans Frontières" mean?	
a. Mediziner sind Frontiere	**b.** Doctors go everywhere
c. Doctors and nurses	**d.** Doctors without borders
Question no. 7: What is the main aim of the Bill and Melinda Gates Foundation?	
a. projects to help children in East Africa and India	**b.** support of democratic structures in Eastern Europe
c. health projects in developing countries	**d.** networking of influential people to find ways of helping

b. Now create your own questions on the issue. Use the texts in your Students' Book or other sources. Then, ask each other in class.

Question no. 8:	
a.	**b.**
c.	**d.**
Question no. 9:	
a.	**b.**
c.	**d.**
Question no. 10:	
a.	**b.**
c.	**d.**

Summit G8, p. 183

13 Irish Aphorisms

Stylistic devices

There are a lot of humorous and revealing aphorisms and quotes by famous Irishmen. Enjoy the following examples and identify the stylistic devices used. → Students' Book, Language Kit, p. 295

1. If one could only teach the English how to talk and the Irish how to listen, society would be quite civilized. *Oscar Wilde (1854–1900, Irish playwright)*

____

2. In Ireland the inevitable never happens and the unexpected constantly occurs. *Sir John Pentland Mahaffy (1839–1919, scholar and tutor of Oscar Wilde)*

____

3. The quiet Irishman is about as harmless as a powder magazine built over a match factory. *James Dunne (born 1989, English football player)*

____

4. Making peace, I have found, is much harder than making war. *Gerry Adams (born 1948, Irish politician)*

____

5. I spent 90 % of my money on women and drink. The rest I wasted. *George Best (1946–2005, Irish football player)*

____

6. All the world's a stage and most of us are desperately unrehearsed.
Sean O'Casey (1880–1964, Irish playwright)

---

7. Aim at heaven and you will get earth thrown in. Aim at earth and you get neither.
C. S. Lewis (1898–1963, Irish poet)

---

8. A wise man should have money in his head, but not in his heart.
Jonathan Swift (1667–1745, Anglo-Irish poet)

---

9. It's not that the Irish are cynical. It's simply that they have a wonderful lack of respect for everything and everybody. *Brendan Behan (1923–1964, Irish poet)*

In a pub in Northern Ireland

14 Summit G8, p. 185

Focus on Facts: Regionalism

Common mistakes

15 mistakes (from the fields of grammar, spelling, vocabulary) have slipped into the following *Focus on Facts* text. Using your lie detector, underline the mistakes and correct them in the margin.
→ Students' Book, Language Kit, p. 307

In political terms, regionalism is a doctrine that focuses in the interests of a particular region or group of regions. The term *region* may refer at a traditionell geographical district, a country subdivision, or an administrative or political unit. As the opposite of unitarization, regionalism is the process of divide a political entity or country into smaller jurisdictions and transfering power from the central gouvernment to the regions. Regionalists usual favour lose federations or confederations over a unitary state with a strong central government. The aim of increasing the region's influence and political power can be achieved from movements for limited forms of autonomy (devolution, states' rights, decentralization) or through stronger measures for a greater degree of autonomy (sovereignty, separatism, independence).

A regionalist party is a political party which has it's base almost entirely in a single region and often promotes autonomy for its region. Examples include Portugal's Madeira branch of the Partido Social Democrata, the Scottish National Party and Plaid Cymru in the United Kingdom, the Lega Nord in Italy, and, to some extent, the Christian Social Union of Bavaria. The latter tries to protect Bavaria's interests against European bodies getting more and more influence.

Proponents bring several arguments for regionalism. To their minds, strengthening a region's governing bodies and political powers within a larger country helps to
- counterbalance centralization, globalisation and immigration,
- support the local population,
- increase efficiency (less waste of time, funds, energy),
- develop a more rational allocation of the region's resources,
- raise competitiveness levels among the regions and ultimately the whole country,
- save taxpayers' money.

Regional identity goes often along with socio-cultural identity. Thus the regionalism also finds expression in literature, e.g. local-colour fiction: Steinbeck (Western US), Chopin (Southern US); architecture, e.g. Sydney Opera House; art, e.g. 1930s rural life paintings by Grant Wood, Iowa; dialect, e.g. Northern English: [u] butler,/æ/dance,/u:/cow.

In some countries, the development of regionalist policies may be a prelude to further demands for greater autonomy or even full seperation, especially when ethnic and cultural disparities are present. This has been demonstrated in the late 1980s in Yugoslavia.

Culture – High and Low

1 For the Love of Analysis

Summit G8, p. 188

Analysing non-fictional texts

Study the non-fictional text on Damien Hirst's piece of art *For the Love of God* again and write at least one sentence each on the following 10 most common aspects of text analysis.
→ Students' Book, Language Kit, p. 302

1. text type
2. heading
3. topic
4. intention
5. structure
6. author's attitude
7. author's competence
8. author's argumentation
9. style
10. tone

Damien Hirst

2 Focus on Facts: Modern Art

Summit G8, p. 190

Identifying art movements

The following table briefly describes important art movements of the last 60 years and lists some outstanding representatives of them. Identify the name of each movement.

name of the movement	representatives	descriptions
1.	Billy Childish, Charles Thomson	art movement founded in 1999 in Britain to promote figurative painting in opposition to conceptual art, formed as an alternative to the Charles Saatchi-patronised Young British Artists
2.	Jackson Pollock, Willem de Kooning	an American post-World War II art movement combining the emotional intensity and self-denial of the German Expressionists with the antifigurative aesthetic of the European abstract schools such as Futurism or the Bauhaus
3.	Marina Abramovic, Youri Messen-Jaschin	art made on the human body, e.g. tattoos, body piercings, branding, scalpelling, shaping, body painting, mutilation, or pushing the body to its physical limits
4.	Mark Rothko, Barnett Newman	abstract style emerging in the 1950s, characterized by abstract canvases painted primarily with large areas of solid color
5.	Andy Goldsworthy, Richard Long	an art movement in which landscape and the work of art are inextricably linked; the works frequently exist in the open, left to change and erosion under natural conditions
6.	Victor Vasarely, Bridget Riley	a genre of visual art, especially painting, making use of optical illusions; also known as optical art or perceptual abstraction

name of the movement	representatives	descriptions
7.	Nam June Paik, Gary Hill	a contemporary art method combining video technology with installation art, utilizing its surrounding environment to affect the audience
8.	Andy Warhol, David Hockney, Keith Haring, Robert Rauschenberg	a visual art movement characterized by themes and techniques drawn from popular mass culture (advertising, comic books), emphasizing the banal or kitschy elements of any given culture
9.	Banksy, Cease	art developed in public spaces, including graffiti artwork, wheatpasting, sticker art, street poster art, video projection, guerrilla art, street installations
10.	Damien Hirst, Tracey Emin	a group of conceptual artists, painters, sculptors and installation artists based in the United Kingdom, noted for "shock tactics", use of throwaway materials and wild living

Meeting a Land Artist

3 Summit G8, p. 190

Mediating

Together with Andy Goldsworthy, Richard Long is one of the most popular land artists. Read the following interview with him and mediate its contents into English guided by the following five questions:

1. Warum bevorzugt Long in seiner Arbeit Einfachheit und Klarheit?
2. Woher nimmt er seine Materialien (*deadwood, mud*)? Warum?
3. Warum will er nicht in Amerika arbeiten?
4. Inwiefern ist er vom Außenseiter zum Etablierten avanciert?
5. Wie fasst er die Geschichte seines eigenen Lebens zusammen?

→ Students' Book, Method Kit, p. 258

art-magazin: In den letzten Jahren ist unter dem Stichwort „LOHAS" der „Lifestyle of Health and Sustainability" zum Massenphänomen geworden, der auch eine bewusste Wahrnehmung der Umwelt einschließt. Die aktuell gezeigten Arbeiten sind zum Teil aus Treibholz und Fundstücken entstanden – sind Sie ein Pionier dieser alten und neuen Öko-Bewegungen?

Richard Long in front of his *River Avon Mud Circle*

Long: Von Natur aus verstehe ich mich eigentlich nicht als politisches Wesen, aber diese Interpretation ist natürlich legitim. Wobei ich damit angefangen habe, bevor es überhaupt das Bewusstsein für Ökologie und „grüne" Politik gab und der Ursprung meiner Beziehung zur Natur auch bestimmte Vorstellungen davon sind, wie ich künstlerisch arbeiten wollte. Zehn Meilen geradeaus und zurück – das geht natürlich am besten in freier Natur, nicht in der Stadt. Und obwohl ich selbst kein Zen-Buddhist bin, sehe ich meine Arbeit als Anregung zu Meditation und Kontemplation und fühle durchaus eine gewisse Nähe zu dieser Philosophie. Dazu leben wir in einer komplexen, um nicht zu sagen chaotischen und von Bildern überfluteten Welt – auf die ich mit einer Kunst reagiere, die einfach und geradeaus ist. Keine Tricks, kein Schnickschnack – sozusagen archaisch. So schlicht wie ein einfacher Fuß- oder Fingerabdruck. Aber dennoch sind auch die einfachsten Formen, jeder Kreis und jede Linie, unterschiedlich, da sich alle Orte auf dem Planeten voneinander unterscheiden. Gerade die einfachen Dinge zeichnen sich durch eine kosmische Vielfalt aus. Weswegen für mich meine Arbeit auch eine ganz persönliche ist, die eben nicht wie bei vielen anderen Künstlern von Assistenten verrichtet wird: Sie misst genau die Zeit, die ich für eine bestimmte Strecke brauche – und niemand anders. Es hat immer mit mir zu tun.

art-Magazin: Woher kommen die Materialien für Ihre Arbeit?

Long: Das Treibholz habe ich an den Ufern des Severn aufgelesen, und auch der Schlamm stammt aus diesem Fluss. Man kann mit ein wenig Schlamm und viel Wasser, große Bilder schaffen – wieder mein Interesse an den praktischen Dingen. Und an dem Ort, an dem ich noch immer lebe und an dem ich noch immer Wanderungen unternehme. Was aber nicht heißt, dass ich jeden Luxus ablehne: Manchmal nehmen mich auch Leute im Privatjet mit. Für mich macht es die Mischung: An einem Tag schlafe ich unter einem Felsen in den Bergen oder in einer Hecke am Straßenrand, am nächsten Tag im Adlon. Wobei mein biografischer Hintergrund eher in den Jugendherbergen der Nachkriegszeit liegt, die ja auch mit idealistischen bis sozialistischen Lebensentwürfen verbunden waren.
Teil meiner Arbeit ist auch die englische Tradition eines öffentlichen Wegerechts, weswegen meine Arbeit so in Amerika nicht entstanden wäre. Es gibt dort viele Orte, an denen man fürs Betreten erschossen werden könnte. [...]

art-Magazin: Als junger Kunststudent wurden Sie aus dem West England College of the Arts im letzten Studienjahr heraus geworfen – heute sind sie Mitglied der Royal West England Academy of the Arts – ein denkbar langer Weg vom Außenseiter zum Etablierten. Nehmen Sie diese Strecke als einen sich schließenden Kreis oder als eine gerade Linie wahr?

Long: Eine Linie – eine langsame. Aber andererseits hatte ich auch in jungen Jahren bereits viel Erfolg und Glück – schon vier Jahre nach dem Rauswurf aus Bristol wurde ich im MoMA ausgestellt. Aber ich bin kein Nomade, wenn eine Wanderung abgeschlossen ist, kehre ich heim. Die Geschichte meines Lebens ist: Aufbruch zu verschiedenen Orten und Rückkehr an denselben Ort – allerdings als anderer Mensch. Berlin und sein Umland werde ich übrigens schon wieder nicht erkunden – ich bin eigentlich ein ganz schlechter Tourist.

from www.art-magazine.de/kunst/7279/richard_long_haunch_of_venison, interview by Gunnar Luetzow [24.09.08]

Summit G8, p. 195

4 "Art and Literature Are Providing Me with Life"

Characteristics of spoken English

Read or – if possible – listen to Frank's turns in the dialogue and identify characteristics of spoken English. → Students' Book, Language Kit, p. 304

Example: What's wrong? (l. 2): *contracted form*

Summit G8, p. 199

5 Writing on Media – Blessing or Curse?

Improving one's style

Isabelle from a Bavarian grammar school, Chiemgau Gymnasium Traunstein (Pope Benedict's former school), wrote the following composition on the topic "Mankind and media – blessing or curse?". Improve on her choice of words by replacing the words in bold type. You find a lot of synonyms in your Thesaurus. → Students' Book, Language Kit, p. 305

There has been heated controversy on the **question** ______________ **(1)** of whether the media **change** ______________ **(2)** society for the better or worse. There are people who think all **kinds** ______________ **(3)** of media are **bad for** ______________ **(4)** us but there are also supporters who do not **like** ______________ **(5)** this **opinion** ______________ **(6)**.

Among the arguments for media as a blessing, one must mention **easy**____________ **(7)** entertainment. When the weather is bad, for example, you can watch **great** ____________ **(8)** movies or play **funny** ____________ **(9)** computer games, so you do not get bored **quickly** ____________ **(10)**. Another argument is **fast** ____________ **(11)** coverage of world affairs as you are **quickly** ____________ **(12)** informed about current events. My last point is that media are an **interesting** ____________ **(13)** invention for personal enrichment and education. You can enlarge your knowledge by **getting** ____________ **(14)** **things** ____________ **(15)** from the Internet, watching **important** ____________ **(16)** films, etc.

Now let me **go on** ____________ **(17)** to the arguments which are **used** ____________ **(18)** against media. I'd like to draw your attention to the fact that many media are **bad for** ____________ **(19)** your health. Lots of children sit in front of the TV set **eating** ____________ **(20)** crisps instead of going outside and doing some **kinds** ____________ **(21)** of sport. Doctors **know** ____________ **(22)** that too many children are overweight. Do you **like** ____________ **(23)** that? Another point is illiteracy as more and more people are forgetting how to read or write. They **think** ____________ **(24)** it is **easier** ____________ **(25)** to watch the news than reading it in **good** ____________ **(26)** newspapers. Another **main** ____________ **(27)** argument is manipulation of viewers by the media. Especially **young people** ____________ **(28)** can easily be influenced by new media as they have not yet found their identities. When they see certain series, for example, they cannot **get** ____________ **(29)** the **right** ____________ **(30)** attitudes. Just look at "Germany's Next Top Model", when Klum & Co. tell the participants they are **very** ____________ **(31)** fat, whereas in reality they are **really** ____________ **(32)** thin. Some girls try to imitate their role models and may become anorexic.

To put it in a nutshell, one may **finish** ____________ **(33)** by saying that media, the 4th power, are **really** ____________ **(34)** a mixed blessing.

Focus on Facts: Media

6 Summit G8, p. 201

Labelling diagrams

a. The following diagram visualizes a model of communication. Fill in the boxes with the proper terms.

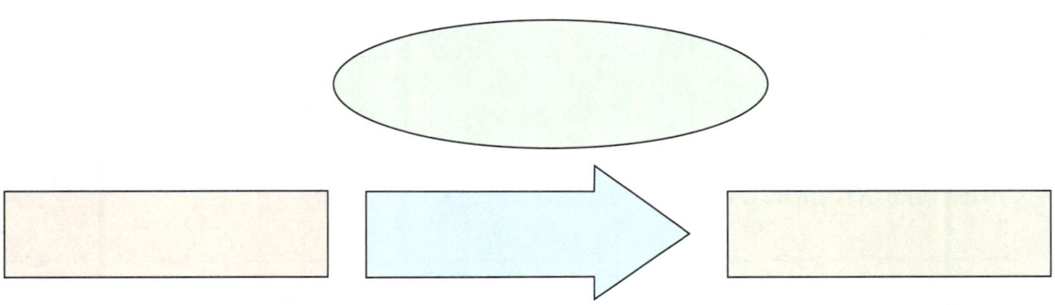

Matching

b. Match the following examples of media with the corresponding forms (types).

examples	forms
feature film	aural/oral media
video installation	print media
website	audio-visual media
newspaper	hypermedia
radio	art media

Definitions

c. Define the following terms:

media literacy: ______________________________

____

ideographic writing: ______________________________

____

information overload: ______________________________

____

Mediating

d. How would you translate *media literacy* and *information overload*?

→ Students' Book, Method Kit, p. 258

Summit G8, p. 205

7 Focus on Facts: Web 2.0

Identifying applications

a. Which Web 2.0 applications do the following websites belong to?

1. http://video.google.com: ______________________________
2. www.schuelervz.net: ______________________________
3. www.wikipedia.org: ______________________________
4. www.podcastsinenglish.com/pages: ______________________________
5. www.usingenglish.com/profiles/tdol: ______________________________

Paraphrasing

b. Paraphrase the following passages from the text without using the words in bold type.

1. The Internet and the World Wide Web **are** not **synonymous**.

____

2. ... one of the services **accessible via** the Internet.

____

3. ... a phrase **coined** by O'Reilly Media ...

____

4. ... which **aim to facilitate collaboration** ...

____

5. ... it has sometimes **sunk** simply **to the status of a marketing buzzword**.

____

Harmless Fun?

8 Summit G8, p. 206

Genre writing

Create an advertisement or leaflet against the use of toy weapons and violent computer games by teenagers. The following words and phrases might be useful:

- violence, gore, and anti-social behaviour
- alternative games increase positive social interaction
- easy access to these games
- repetition and rewards increase learning
- exposure to violent games increases aggressive thoughts, emotions and actions
- world without war
- harmful
- conflict
- ultra violent games inappropriate for all children
- harmless fun
- adventurous
- more likely to fight as adults
- teenagers more likely to imitate the actions of a character
- inappropriate for young players
- active participation rather than passive observation
- increasingly realistic and exciting nature of electronic games
- banned toy guns
- It's our task as parents to protect our children.
- point of view of the shooter

Focus on Facts: Shakespeare's Language

9 Summit G8, p. 214

Finding omitted words

In the following text, five important words/phrases have been omitted. Mark the spots and write the missing words in the margin.

When we read Shakespeare, we are confronted with the modern period of English. As far as grammar and spelling were concerned, his language was not as fixed as today. The Saxon vocabulary of Old English was hugely increased with Latin and French loanwords. Shakespeare was able to draw on his education at *King Edward VI Grammar School for Boyes* where Greek were given special emphasis. He also profited from the structural flexibility and verbal inventiveness of the Elizabethan language. There was hardly any limit to creating new words or playing with meanings. So he could create wonderful dialogues and sonnets. One of his most famous sonnets is No. 18: *Shall I compare thee to a day?*

All the World's ... an Analysis

10 Summit G8, pp. 215–224

In Shakespeare's pastoral comedy *As You Like It*, Duke Senior, the rightful ruler of the dukedom in which the play is set, realizes that there are a lot of conflicts in the world. Jaques, one of his faithful lords, who follows him into exile in the Forest of Arden, replies with these famous lines.

Read the lines and analyse them by answering the questions on the next page.

Text analysis

All the world's a stage,
And all the men and women merely players:
They have their exits and their entrances;
And one man in his time plays many parts,
His acts being seven ages. At first the infant,
Mewling[1] and puking in the nurse's arms.
And then the whining school-boy, with his satchel
And shining morning face, creeping like snail
Unwillingly to school. And then the lover,

[1] **mewling** crying like a cat

Sighing like furnace, with a woeful ballad
Made to his mistress' eyebrow. Then a soldier,
Full of strange oaths and bearded like the pard[2],
Jealous in honour, sudden and quick in quarrel,
Seeking the bubble reputation
Even in the cannon's mouth. And then the justice,
In fair round belly with good capon[3] lined,
With eyes severe and beard of formal cut,
Full of wise saws[4] and modern instances[5],
And so he plays his part. The sixth age shifts
Into the lean and slipper'd pantaloon[6],
With spectacles on nose and pouch[7] on side,
His youthful hose, well saved, a world too wide
For his shrunk shank[8]; and his big manly voice,
Turning again toward childish treble, pipes
And whistles in his sound. Last scene of all,
That ends this strange eventful history,
Is second childishness and mere oblivion,
Sans teeth, sans eyes, sans taste, sans everything.

William Shakespeare: *As You Like It*, II. 7

The progression of an upper class gentleman through life

[2]**pard** leopard – [3]**capon** *(arch.)* chicken – [4]**wise saws** proverbs – [5]**modern instances** dull examples – [6]**pantaloon** here: silly old man – [7]**pouch** purse – [8]**shrunk shank** thin leg

a. Comprehension

Summarize in one sentence what this speech is about.

b. Analysis

- Which of these four stylistic devices does the speaker use in the first line: simile – personification – metaphor – hyperbole?
  → Language Kit, pp. 295 ff.
- How is the seventh age characterized?
- Choose one simile from the text and explain its function.
  → Language Kit, p. 297
- Which outlook on life does Jaques, the speaker, display here: optimistic, melancholy, overjoyed, pessimistic, down-to-earth?

c. Production

Choose one age and rewrite it so that it sounds positive.

Example: First age: At first the infant,
Protected and pampered by loving mother,
Looked at and admired by everybody,
Innocent and unaware of worldly affairs.

Summit G8, p. 224

11 Bottom's Up

Finding rhyming words

The following lines are taken from Humphrey Carpenter's parodies called *Shakespeare Without the Boring Bits*. They form the beginning of Bottom's drunken rap as he tells of his *Midsummer Night's Dream*. Try to guess the missing rhyming words (pair rhyme).

BOTTOM: Now, someone buy me another drink,
And I'll tell you a tale that'll make you ________________ (1)
Of how, though I am fat and ________________ (2)
I was chatted up by a bloomin' fairy.

ALL: Good old Bottom, buy him a half,
He may be a buttock but he makes us ________________ (3)

BOTTOM: It was for the royal wedding day
That our drama club rehearsed a ________________ (4)
A bit of a show for the Duke and his bride,
Out of doors if fine, if it rained, ________________ (5)
Peter Quince, who works on a building site
Was our producer, and we met one ________________ (6)
To work out who was going to play what.
Now as an actor I'm pretty ________________ (7)
I can throw my voice like a kiddie's ________________ (8)
Well, we were doing Pyramus and Thisby.
The story's a bit like Romeo and ________________ (9)
About a girl who hasn't left school yet.
The bloke who loves her thinks she's dead,
So he goes and chops off his bloomin' ________________ (10)
We didn't argue who would ________________ (11)
I was the one whose career would go far.
It's true that I work in a clothing ________________ (12)
But just look at me – you can see I'm actory.

Humphrey Carpenter: *Shakespeare Without the Boring Bits*, London, Viking, 1994, pp. 46 f.

Dire Straits: Romeo and Juliet

18 CD2

12 Summit G8, p. 229

Listening comprehension

In the following gapped text, not only have single words been deleted but also chunks (phrases, idioms, etc.). While listening to *Romeo and Juliet* by Dire Straits, fill in the gaps.

A lovestruck Romeo sings a streetsuss serenade
________________________ (1) with a love song that he made
Finds a streetlight, steps out of the shade
Says something like you and me babe, ________________ (2)?

Juliet says hey, it's Romeo, you nearly gimme ____________ (3)
He's underneath the window, she's singing hey la my boyfriend's back
You shouldn't ____________ (4) singing up at people like that
Anyway what you gonna do about it?

Juliet, the dice was loaded ____________ (5)
And I bet that you exploded in my heart
And I forget, I forget the movie song
When you gonna realize it was just that ____________ (6), Juliet?

Come up on different streets, they both were streets of shame
Both dirty, both mean, yes and the dream was ____________ (7)
And I dreamed your dream for you and now your dream is real
How can you look at me as if I was just another ____________ (8)?

When you can fall for chains of silver, you can ____________ (9) chains of gold
You can fall for pretty strangers and the promises they hold
You promised me everything, you promised me ____________ (10), yeah
Now you just say oh Romeo, yeah, you know I used to have a scene with him

Juliet, when ____________ (11), you used to cry
You said I love you like the stars above, said I'll love you till I die
____________ (12) for us you know the movie song
When you gonna realize it was just that the time was wrong, Juliet?

I can't do the talk like they talk on TV
And I can't do a love song like the way ____________ (13)
I can't do everything, but I'd do anything for you
I can't do anything except ____________ (14) with you

And all I do is miss you and the way we used to be
All I do is ____________ (15) and bad company
Now all I do is kiss you through the bars of a rhyme
Juliet, I'd do the stars with you ____________ (16)

Juliet, when we made love you used to cry ...

A lovestruck Romeo sings a streetsuss serenade ...

Teenage Views of the Bard

13 Summit G8, pp. 213–234

The following text summarizes a few howlers secondary school pupils produced when they had to answer questions about Shakespeare in national exams.

Put the infinitives in brackets into participles or gerunds and decide whether you have to use present or past.

-ing forms, present and past

Romeo, ________________ **(to accord/1)** to one 14-year-old ___________ **(to sit/2)** his Shakespeare test, drowned on the Titanic. Another teenager, ______________ **(to ask/3)** to explain Shakespeare's ________________ **(to handle/4)** of the balcony scene in Romeo and Juliet, said: "They jump in the swimming pool."

These are just some of the howlers _____________ **(to make/5)** by secondary school pupils ________________ **(to answer/6)** questions about Shakespeare in national curriculum tests for 14-year-olds. The first respondent had obviously confused Leonardo DiCaprio's _____________ **(to star/7)** roles in *Romeo and Juliet* and *Titanic*. The second pupil had taken Luhrmann's modern version ___________ **(to set/8)** in a Los Angeles apartment block with swimming pool as gospel.

Apart from ________________ **(to confuse/9)** text and film, the pupils have also made efforts to use teenspeak in ________________________ **(to explain/10)** the great man's works, even __________________ **(to add/11)** a sprinkling of drugs and sex. For instance, Macbeth, _______________ **(to hear/12)** of his wife's death, "goes into full-on soliloquy mode[1]." Another pupil adds that Lady Macbeth, after Duncan ____________________ **(to be murdered/13)**, "ses to Macbeth 'sort your head out'[2]". A third pupil spoke of Lady Macbeth _______________ **(to ask/14)** her husband "to show her his manhood[3]". In one essay ______________ **(to write/15)** as part of a classroom exercise before the test, a pupil dealt with Macbeth __________ **(to see/16)** the three witches by saying: "Macbeth had been smoking up[4] and imaged[5] them all."

Past GCSE exams include one student _________________ **(to believe/17)** that Miguel Cervantes, a contemporary of Shakespeare's, wrote the book *Donkey Hote*[6], and _________________ **(to go/18)** on to state: "The next great author was John Milton. Milton wrote *Paradise Lost*. Then his wife died and he wrote *Paradise Regained*[7]."

Another howler _________________ **(to take/19)** from an earlier GCSE exam said: "Shakespeare wrote tragedies, comedies and hysterectomies[8] – all in Islamic[9] pentameter." A second wrote that Caesar had been murdered by the Ides of March and that his _________________ **(to die/20)** words were "same to you, Brutus".

---

[1]**full-on soliloquy mode** *(infml.) „voller Selbstgesprächsmodus"* – [2]**to sort out one's head** *(infml.) sich klar werden* – [3]**manhood** *Männlichkeit, (euph.) Penis* – [4]**to smoke up** *(Joint) fertig rauchen* – [5]**to image** *(infml.) sich einbilden* [6]**Donkey Hote** = **Don Quixote** (**donkey** = *Esel*) – [7]**to regain** *wiederfinden* – [8]**hysterectomy** *Gebärmutterentfernung (gemeint war:* histories) – [9]**Islamic** *gemeint war:* **iambic**

Summit G8, pp. 216–224

14 Bloody Bard

C-test

In the following newspaper report about a health warning issued by the Globe Theatre, the second half of every second word is missing. Try to fill the gaps in this so-called C-test.

Watching Shakespeare plays can be more dangerous than one may assume. The Lon_ _ _ Globe The_ _ _ _ has iss_ _ _ a health war_ _ _ _ after fo_ _ people coll_ _ _ _ _ during a produ_ _ _ _ _ of *Titus Andronicus*. The Ba_ _ _ bloodiest pl_ _ shows sce_ _ _ of ra_ _ and mur_ _ _. Its mo_ _ famous sc_ _ _ comes wh_ _ the Qu_ _ _ is ser_ _ _ a p_ _ filled wi_ _ the coo_ _ _ flesh o_ her o_ _ sons. But i_ was t_ _ horrific sce_ _ in wh_ _ _ Lavinia has h_ _ hands c_ _ off a_ _ tongue c_ _ out th_ _ proved t_ _ gruesome f_ _ the groun_ _ _ _ _ _, the audi_ _ _ _ members w_ _ stand i_ the Ya_ _.

Summit G8, pp. 213–234

15 All the Words … for the Sage

Let's repeat 18 words from the chapter.

Vocabulary training

a. There are three columns for each word: the first is the English word, the second an English definition, and the third the German equivalent. Fill in the missing parts.

English word	English definition	German equivalent
	poem of 14 lines	
	part of a song	
	person who writes plays	*Dramatiker*
	the last few words of a humorous story, joke	
to resemble	to look like	
to brag		*angeben*
	person who is addressed	*Adressat, Zielpublikum*
soliloquy		*Monolog, Selbstgespräch*

English word	English definition	German equivalent
	tired/sick of sth.	*überdrüssig*
satire		
		Liebesgeschichte
		Strumpfhose
	to set one's foot down	*gehen, treten*
	impossible to explain by natural causes	*übernatürlich*
ambition	a strong desire to achieve sth.	
		auf den ersten Blick
tragedy		
(infml.)	to be tricked into believing sth. which is not true	*hereinfallen*

b. Memorize these 18 words by making use of the traditional vocabulary learning method, i.e. covering one or two columns with a sheet of paper and saying the hidden words out loud.

c. In what ways does the illustration reflect Shakespeare's two lines?

"All the world's a stage,
And all the men and women merely players ..."
William Shakespeare, As You Like It, Act II, Scene VII

English Around the World

Summit G8, p. 238

1 Learning English: The Rise in Demand

Analysing statistics and graphs

This graph gives estimates for both past and future potential demand for English in the educational systems of the world. To this end, it shows the estimated numbers of English language learners (in millions) over a timespan of nearly 100 years.

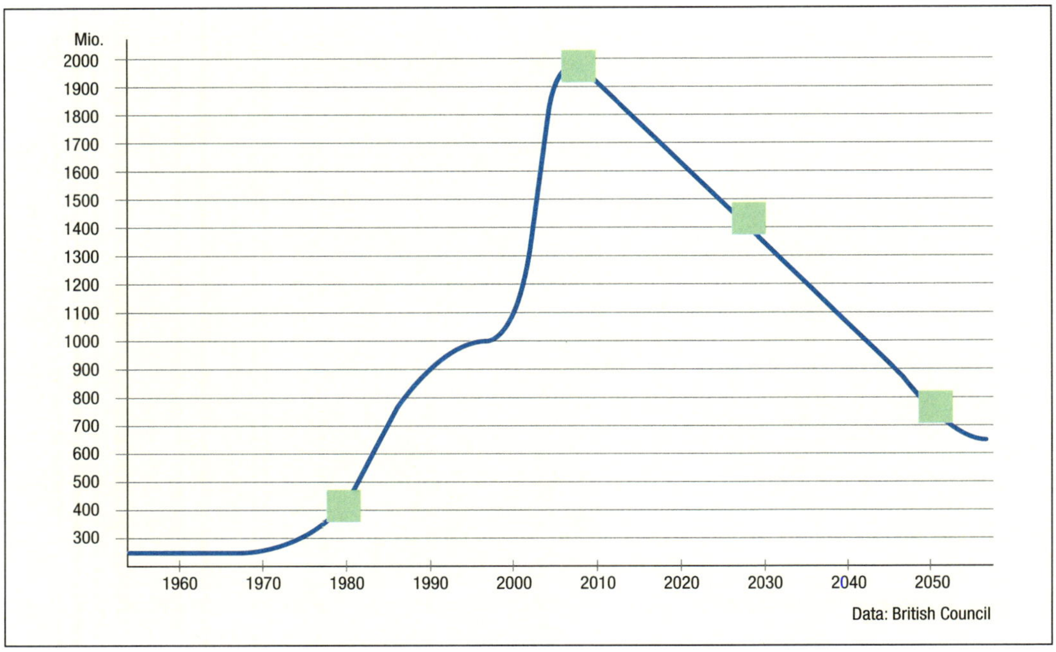

Fill in the missing words in the correct form and match the following statements with their appropriate position in the graph.

cradle	primary	to decline	majority	pattern	to represent	
rapid	to slow	steady	to reach	to study	to take off	peak

A The model suggests a basic ______ (1) of ______ (2) growth in the 1970s and 1980s, ______ (3) in the early 1990s and then ______ (4) again at the end of the 20th century.

B The number of learners will ______ (5) as cohorts of children who have studied English at ______ (6) school reach secondary and tertiary study.

C If the *World English Project* is successful, then eventually a ______ (7) state will be ______ (8) where the ______ (9) of learners are either young, or in need of specialist support.

D The ______ (10) of the graph ______ (11) the point at which learners of all ages will be ______ (12) English – from ______ (13) to grave.

Focus on Facts: Global Language

2 Summit G8, p. 240

True or false?

a. Decide whether the following statements are right or wrong. Correct the wrong ones.

1. The main reasons for the dominance of the English language today are the role of the British Empire and the influence of the USA.
2. English is the language which most people in the world speak as their first language.
3. English is the No. 1 language because on the one hand, no other language has more native and non-native speakers, and on the other, it is scattered around the whole world (in contrast to Chinese).
4. A *lingua franca* is a language which native speakers use when communicating with non-natives.
5. There is no single English language, but many *Englishes*.
6. When two peoples with different languages are engaged in trade, pidgin English may develop.
7. Creole is similar to pidgin, but it is more stable.
8. BBC English is not a dialect, but the standard of British English.
9. American English, British English and Australian English are the three major branches of English.
10. South African English is a sub-type of British English.

Discussion

b. Discuss the four issues which are listed towards the end of p. 240 in your Students' Book. Which side are you on in each case?

Understanding the Germans

3 Summit G8, p. 241

Mediating: explaining difficult words (circumlocution)

Imagine you are with an American exchange student and you come across the following words during his/her stay in Germany:

Raumbelegungsplan	Schienenersatzverkehr	Kostümzwang	Solidaritätszuschlag
Bundesverfassungsgericht	Vertretungsstunde	Jugendschutzgesetz	Sperrstunde

Choose at least three of the words, make a few notes and then explain them in one sentence each.
→ Students' Book, Method Kit, p. 258

The English Language Is Taking Over the World. But Should We Rejoice?

4 Summit G8, p. 242

Vocabulary training

Read the text on p. 242 in your Students' Book attentively and then find alternative expressions or synonyms for the phrases in bold type.

1. something they were so **hungry for** (l. 12)

____

2. **cultural and linguistic "biodiversity"** (l. 21)

____

____

3. [...] Native Americans have **suffered immeasurably** as a result of these all too real **culture wars.** (ll. 26 f.)

____

____

4. [...] the local Africans who were (to our shame) the **underpaid servants and maids** in the homes. (ll. 30 f.)

____

____

5. to **replant their roots** (l. 47)

____

____

6. One of my most **painful memories** is being thrown out of a sports shop [...]. (l. 54)

____

____

Summit G8, p. 244

5 Focus on Facts: Word Formation in English

Word formation

Choose three types of word formation, e. g. coining, back-formation, etc. and add at least five more examples using an English-English dictionary and/or the Internet (i. e. www.wikipedia.com; www.wiktionary.com).

type of word formation	examples
______________________	1. ______________ 2. ______________ 3. ______________ 4. ______________ 5. ______________
______________________	1. ______________ 2. ______________ 3. ______________ 4. ______________ 5. ______________
______________________	1. ______________ 2. ______________ 3. ______________ 4. ______________ 5. ______________

Moving On

Applying for a Job

1 Summit G8, p. 250

Job application strategies

One of the options for life after school may be to earn your own money "Down Under". You can look for a job with the help of the Internet. Here are some examples of what you can find there:

Retail
Work is available in department stores, boutiques and specialty stores. Most positions are as sales assistants, however, there are also stocktaking jobs. For retail you need excellent English and most employers prefer some experience. Jobs are easier to obtain in the months leading up to Christmas – particularly in department stores. At other times of the year, it's more difficult as employers prefer permanent staff. You'll need fluent English and a friendly manner. Sales and cash register experience will also help.

Au Pair/Nanny
Live-in with a family and work several hours a day caring for children and assisting with house work. Depending on the number of hours, you can earn $150 – $200 per week + accommodation and meals. The experience of living with a family will give you insight into Australian culture and there are positions available in both cities and rural areas.

Volunteer in the 'Outback' of the world's most ecologically diverse continent. Isolated for 55 million years, Australia evolved as a sanctuary to species long since extinct elsewhere. It is an extreme environment, and it needs our help.
Globalisation and the effects of climate change have left Australia in great need of conservationists – battling drought and deforestation. If you want to get away from civilization for a while and protect our bioheritage, join us in an i-to-i Venture in Australia.

Fruit picking
Harvesting fruit and vegetables is popular with travellers. There is harvest work somewhere in Australia most of the year. However, it is hard, physical work and often in hot weather. Farmers sometimes pay by the hour, but most pay by the amount you pick – so you'll earn more as you gain experience. You will need to protect yourself from the sun with a broad rimmed hat, long sleeved shirt and sunscreen.

Call centres
If you have sales experience and love to talk – this could be the job for you. Most positions involve cold calling over the phone to sell a product. You will need to have a native level of English and be confident about your sales skills. Positions are usually for 2–3 months and pay is approximately $16 per hour + bonuses for sales.

Farm work
A great way to experience the Australian 'Outback'. You will be helping around the farm, fencing, driving tractors or looking after stock. Wages vary according to the job and experience. Most farms include meals and accommodation. As it can be difficult to find farm work with no farming experience, many AIFS participants do a farm course beforehand that covers basic skills like horse riding, shearing sheep, rounding up cattle and mending fences. The course organizers then refer you to farm jobs around Australia. The courses and jobs are available year round, except for a few weeks over our Christmas/Summer break, if you're prepared to travel the distance.

a. Having read the job offers, collect application strategies. Consider the form, topic and style of a good application and add these to the grid.

A good application should ...	A good application should NOT ...
be addressed to the right person in charge.	*contain colloquialisms.*
...	...

b. Choose one of the advertised jobs and apply for it. Think of your CV, too.
→ Students' Book, Method Kit, p. 278

Acknowledgements

Illustrations

front cover: © Ute Grabowsky/photothek.net, Foto: Michael Zegers; back cover: © F1 ONLINE www.f1online.de; p. 4, 38 bottom, 39: Reinhild Kassing/Verlagsarchiv Schöningh; p. 9, 22: Martin Kohn/Verlagsarchiv Schöningh; p. 13: © Copyright 2008 Pat Bagley; p. 14: AP Photo/Fiona Hanson/Pool; p. 16: © picture-alliance/dpa; p. 17: taken from Orhan Pamuk: Snow, Faber & Faber, London 2004; p. 18: John Giles/AP; p. 19: Mansell/Time Pix/Rex Features; p. 20: Charles Moore - Black Star; p. 21: picture-alliance/ZUMA Press; p. 24: © VG Bild-Kunst, Bonn 2010; p. 25: Copyright © 2005 Greta Pratt; p. 27: The Economist, February 15th-21st, 2003; p. 28: Carmen Mendez/Verlagsarchiv Schöningh; p. 29: Keystone; p. 30: privat; p. 34: www.CartoonStock.com; p. 35: Kipper Williams; p. 36 top: Martin Honeysett; p. 36 bottom: © IPN/Caleb Kenna; p. 37: taken from Jodi Picoult: Nineteen Minutes, London, Hodder & Stoughton 2008; p. 38 top: J.J. für wikipedia.org; p. 41: © OKAPIA; p. 42: © Copyright 2008 John Darkow; p. 43: © IPN/Dennis Brack; p. 45 top: © Copyright 2008 Jiho – All Rights Reserved; p. 47 top: © dieKLEINERT.de/ Martin Guhl; p. 47 bottom: Honda; p. 48 top left: Schwalme/CCC, www.c5.net; p. 48 top right: not traceable; p. 48 bottom: student's work; p. 50: Ron Barrett; p. 52, Solutions p. 19: © Andy Singer; p. 53 top left: terre des hommes; p. 53 top right: © Jonas Ekströmer; p. 55: © Olaf Meinhardt/ transit-Archiv; p. 56, 57: © picture-alliance/dpa; p. 62: Drawing by Henry Martin © 1987 The New Yorker Magazine; p. 63: taken from: Humphrey Carpenter: Shakespaere Without the Boring Bits. London: Penguin 1994, Illustrations: The Big i, 1994; p. 64: © picture-alliance/schroewig; p. 66: Photograph: John Haynes; p. 67: taken from http://www.absolutely-intercultural.com/?p=116; Solutions p. 22 from top left to bottom right: © picture-alliance/dpa, © picture-alliance/dpa, © vario images, © Petra Steuer/JOKER

Every effort has been made to supply complete copyright information for the pictures included here. Should such entries be incomplete or contain errors, we request copyright owners to contact the publishers so that we can proceed with the necessary corrections.

Solutions

Stepping In

1 p. 4

b. The first 4 jokes are based on puns, homonyms and homophones: "to serve" – bedienen/servieren, auftischen; "dressing": Tragen/Anziehen von Kleidung, Salatdressing/Kräutersoße für Salat; "watch" – Wache/Bewachung, Uhr, "bear" = Bär, "bare" = nackt. No. 5 refers to the fact that the mother does not know William Shakespeare but thinks he is one of her son's friends.

2 p. 4

German	English	can be mistaken for ...
Brieftasche	wallet	briefcase – *Aktentasche*
Chef	boss	chef – *Koch*
Folie (f. OHP)	transparency	foil – *Alufolie*
Mappe/Hefter	folder	map – *Landkarte*
Mörder	murderer	murder – *Mord*
Minze	mint	to mince – *zerkleinern*
mobben	to bully	mob – *der Pöbel*
Handy	mobile	handy – *praktisch, handlich, nützlich*
Gift	poison	gift – *Geschenk*
Lektüre	reading	lecture – *Vortrag, Vorlesung*
Roman	novel	Roman – *Römer/in, römisch*
prägnant	concise	pregnant – *schwanger*
Personal	staff, personnel	personal – *persönlich*
Rezept (Verschreibung Arzt)	prescription	recipe – *Rezept (Kochen)* receipt – *Quittung*
Lyrik	poetry	lyrics – *Liedtexte*
Hose	trousers	hose – *Schlauch*
Stoff (Textil)	material, fabric	stuff – *Zeug, Kram*
Tablett	tray	tablet – *Tablette*
Wand	wall	wand – *Zauberstab*

Tracing National Identities – Cool Britannia and America Dreaming

p. 6 **1**

1 b: expat: a person living in a country that is not their own; **2 c:** to conjure sth. up: to make sth. appear as a picture in your mind; **3 e:** self-effacement: desire to not attract attention to yourself or your abilities; **4 f:** to cling: to hold on tightly to sb./sth.; **5 g:** trait: a particular quality in your personality; **6 i:** subservient (to sb./sth.): too willing to obey other people; **7 k:** to cane: to hit a child with a cane as a punishment; **8 d:** to slash: to make a long cut with a sharp object; **9 a:** clotted cream: a type of thick cream; **10 l:** indigenous: belonging to a particular place rather than coming to it from somewhere else; **11 m:** to detest: to hate sb./sth. very much; **12 h:** notion: an idea, a belief or an understanding of sth.; **13 j:** dash of eccentricity: a small amount of strangeness

p. 6 **2**

a.

quote	modern English equivalent	quote	modern English equivalent
Heaven's command	God's instruction	shalt	shall
azure	blue	dread	fear
main	sea	thy	your
charter	constitution	woe	trouble
strain	melody	thine	yours
Britons	the British	renown	reputation
blest	blessed	commerce	business and economy
thee	you (obj. case)	repair	go
thou	you (subj. case)		

b. When Great Britain first rose from the blue ocean because God wanted it to be like this, the following words were her constitution and angels sang its melody: Great Britain will dominate the oceans and British people will never be slaves.
Other nations, which are not as blessed as you are, will each be ruled by tyrants some day while you will grow and be successful.
You will be great and free and the others will fear and envy you.
Wars with foreign countries will make you only more majestic and more dreadful: just as loud thunder cannot uproot British oaks but will only make them rooted more deeply.
Conceited tyrants will never defeat you and all their attempts to suppress you will only make you stronger, will trouble them and will make you more famous.
You will govern the countryside, and the economy in your cities will be successful: you will dominate the oceans and all their coastlines.
The fine arts, which are always important in countries where there is freedom, will come to your country: blessed island, in you one finds beauty and also men who are ready to guard it.

p. 7 **3**

had been brought out: past perfect simple, passive – one action had been completed before another action; agent is unknown or unimportant
handcuffed, passed, fixed, lashed: simple past, active: successive actions – one action was completed before another action started
is waiting: present progressive, active: action is in progress at present moment of speaking

had gone – stopped short: past perfect simple, active, simple past, active: one action had been completed before another action was completed
straightens: simple present, active: action happens repeatedly, regularly or as a habit
was fixed: past simple, passive; **began:** past simple, active – two actions in the past that occurred more or less simultaneously, focus is on the noose rather than the agent
has passed off: present perfect simple, active: action completed in the past but has present results

4 p. 8

The British Empire: British West Indies, largest empire in history, 19th and early 20th centuries (dominions, colonies, dependencies, trust territories, protectorates, the British Isles, British North America, British Guiana, British West Africa, British East Africa, India) Australia and New Zealand
The Commonwealth today: world peace, human rights, framework of common values and goals, free trade, equality of women (promoting democracy, universal access to education, good governance, the rule of law, social development)

5 p. 8

a. (1) accident; (2) popular; (3) originated; (4) tennis; (5) set of rules; (6) athletic games; (7) codify; (8) essential part; (9) heritage; (10) Englishness

b. Recherche auf englischsprachigen Internetseiten, anschließend kurze Erklärung der Regeln auf Deutsch

6 p. 9

a.

noun	adjective	noun in German
posterity	posterior	*Nachwelt*
science	scientific	*Wissenschaft*
vigour	vigorous	*Vitalität*
industry	industrial/industrious	*Industrie*
labour	laborious	*Arbeit(skraft)*
gratitude	grateful	*Dankbarkeit*

b.

adjective	noun	adjective in German
equal	equality	*gleichberechtigt*
strong	strength	*stark*
exuberant	exuberance	*überschwänglich*
despotic	despot/despotism	*machthaberisch*
mighty	might	*mächtig*
voluntary	volunteer	*freiwillig*

c.
1. as he is welcomed
2. will from this point onwards develop different features
3. the benefits he gets for his hard work
4. that in the past asked for but did not receive
5. he thus has to think of fresh alternatives

7
p. 10

a.

1. the idea that even the poorest person can end up being successful and leading a wealthy life
2. love of your country and willingness to defend it; national pride
3. a feeling that good things will happen or sth. will be successful
4. a society in which all people have the same rights and the opportunity to reach their aims
5. everybody has the right to live a happy life
6. rights that cannot be taken away from people
7. imaginary borderline between those areas that had already been settled and those that were still considered wild and uncivilized
8. a Calvinist value system that stresses the moral value of work, self-discipline, and individual responsibility as the means to improving one's economic well-being

8
p. 11

(1) tangible; (2) phenomenon; (3) history; (4) ideology; (5) simplest; (6) movement; (7) concepts; (8) beliefs; (9) culture; (10) expansion; (11) territories; (12) overspread; (13) possess; (14) Providence; (15) liberty; (16) rallying; (17) torch

9
p. 12

We ~~never will~~ **will never** (word order: adverb of frequency before main verb or after the first auxiliary) be able to prevent ~~the~~ **a** (indefinite article because the group is mentioned in the text for the first time) small group of misfits from || ~~planing~~ **planning** (doubling of consonants in one-syllable cvc verbs) some ~~terible~~ **terrible** (spelling) act of terror. No matter how far-seeing || and competent our ~~intellegence~~ **intelligence** (spelling) and ~~law-enforcement~~ **law-enforcement** (spelling) officials, || ~~peoples~~ **people** (a people/peoples = Volk/Völker; a person/people = Person/Menschen) will always be able to slip ~~throu~~ **through** (spelling) the cracks in a large, || open and diverse ~~countrie~~ **country** (a country/countries but a boy/boys; change of -y into -ie in plural words after consonant + -y). The real test ~~from~~ **of** (preposition) American || leadership is not ~~weather~~ **whether** (wrong word/spelling) we can make 100 ~~procent~~ **percent** (spelling) sure we || prevent the ~~attak~~ **attack** (spelling; but ATTAC! = anti-globalisation movement) but rather how we ~~response~~ **respond** (noun used instead of verb) to it. Stephen || Flynn, a homeland-security ~~experte~~ **expert** (spelling) ~~in~~ **at** (preposition) the Council on Foreign || Relations, ~~argue~~ **argues** (3rd person singular -s) that our goal should be resilience – how ~~quick~~ **quickly** (adverb with verbs of action) || ~~we can~~ **can we** (word order in questions) bounce back from a disruption? In the ~~materiels~~ **materials** (spelling) || sciences, he ~~point~~ **points** (3rd person singular -s) out, resilience is the ability ~~from~~ **of** (preposition) a material to || recover ~~it's~~ **its** (it's = it is; its = possessive determiner) original shape after ~~the~~ **a** (indefinite article because it is not a special and definite action that was mentioned before in the text) deformation. If one day || bombs do go ~~of~~ **off** (spelling), we must ensure that they cause ~~so~~ **as** (comparison) little || disruption – ~~economical~~ **economic** (false friend/wrong word: economical = sparsam), social, political – ~~how~~ **as** (comparison with "as ... as" = so ... wie) possible. This || would deprive the terrorist ~~from~~ **of** (verb + preposition: deprive of) his main objective. If we ~~will not be~~ **are** || **not terrorized** (passive voice in the present tense in an if-clause), ~~than~~ **then** (spelling/wrong word) in a crucial sense we ~~defeated~~ **have defeated** (Present Perfect instead of Simple Past as the result is important and has an effect in the present time) terrorism. [...]

10
p. 13

(1) of; (2) in; (3) of; (4) to; (5) about; (6) of; (7) with; (8) about; (9) of; (10) about; (11) in/at; (12) to; (13) of; (14) of; (15) to; (16) at; (17) of; (18) with; (19) of; (20) to; (21) to; (22) for/of; (23) with; (24) to; (25) on

Public Life and Political Culture

1 p. 14

In the photo we see Queen Elizabeth II on the occasion of one of her public meetings. Together with her husband, Prince Philipp, who can scarcely be seen behind her in the picture, she is walking along a fence that separates the royal couple from a crowd of waiting and greeting people. As there are Canadian flags pinned on the fence, it can be supposed that the Queen, as the Head of the Commonwealth, is visiting Canada.
The Queen wears a creamy white dress with a suitable hat and looks very fashionable and elegant. Opposite her, behind the fence, there is a smiling elderly man offering her a bunch of violet flowers. The man wears a shirt and a hat with the pattern of the British flag on them. The man's outfit makes a wonderfully comic contrast to the Queen's appearance. His pride and admiration for his former mother country are obvious. This impression is underlined by his slightly bowing gesture, maybe to appear shorter than the Queen. Elizabeth II is smiling too. She seems to enjoy her popularity and the loyalty of her subjects.

2 p. 14

a. (1) published; (2) occasion; (3) provides, (4) value; (5) compared; (6) amount; (7) bar chart; (8) third; (9) agricultural; (10) rose; (11) penny; (12) pence; (13) pie chart; (14) doubled; (15) indicate; (16) incomes

b. The other numbers given show the development of British society. For example, the fifth chart represents the percentage of babies born outside marriage. Whereas more than 50 years ago only a small minority of 3.5 % of all babies were born by unmarried women, by 2000 the percentage had increased to 40 %. This development is paralleled by the percentage of partners in first marriages who lived together beforehand rather than waiting until after their wedding day. Whereas in 1952 there were only 5 % of such partners, in 2000 an overwhelming majority of 70 % had lived together before marrying. Evidently, this change can be interpreted as a sign of liberalism as well as emancipation. On the other hand, family life seems to have lost its attraction. Fifty years ago, 1.5 million people lived on their own instead of in families, compared to 7 million at the beginning of our century. If we correlate these numbers with the percentage of trips made by car, van or taxi that nearly tripled within the space of half a century, it could be concluded that loneliness and the loss of family bonds is the price that modern society has had to pay for mobility, flexibility and freedom of choice. One of the pie charts indicates that life has become more secure in terms of the percentage of crimes solved by the police that had increased from 24 % to 47 %. However, due to widespread negative media coverage, people very often get the opposite impression. Finally, statistics show that women have succeeded in gaining more powerful positions in society. Within the space of 50 years, the number of female Members of Parliament in the UK rose from 17 to 118. Compared to the total number of 646 MPs, women are still not adequately represented in the British legislative branch, but at least, the situation has much improved.

c. The pie charts given represent the numbers in a rather unusual way because they do not refer to a total of 100 percent but try to visualize the relation between the numbers of the year 1952 and those of 2001. So, the number of 47 % in pie chart 9 is larger than the usual 50 %, half of a pie chart. This makes only sense if we see the 47 % in contrast to the 24 % in 2001. We can only speculate why TIME magazine chose this form of presenting numbers. One reason might be simply not to show the numbers in bar charts only.

p. 16 **3**

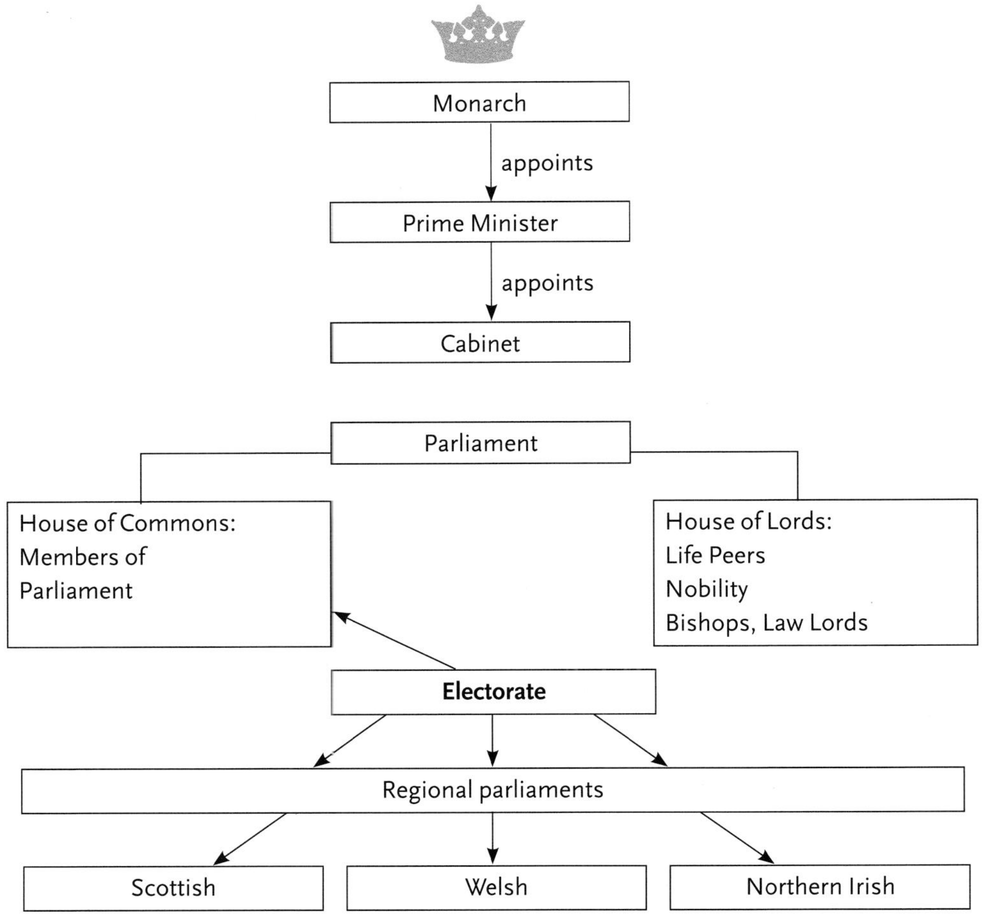

p. 16 **4**

a. 1b; 2a; 3c; 4b; 5c; 6c; 7b

b. to feel embarrassed: to feel awkward, shy or ashamed
to allude to sth.: to mention sth. in an indirect way
to provide a pretext for sth.: to give a false reason for doing sth.
to appreciate sth./sb.: to recognize the good qualities
to endure sth.: to experience and deal with sth. that is unpleasant
to take offense of sth.: to feel attacked
to feel compelled to do sth.: to feel forced

c. Blue supposes that there is only one Western point of view because he sees only one Eastern point of view, too. That is why he has difficulties to understand that the publisher Hans Hansen will want to have printed Blue's biographical details as well as opinions of other people on the issue in question. Blue supposes that being the most prominent Islamist in Turkey he has the right to speak for all Islamic people in Turkey. Ka tries to explain that in Western countries people have an opinion of their own and that is why there are always different points of views. As the media are required to work politically independently and not to take any sides, a well-known newspaper such as the *Frankfurter Rundschau* would not publish a one-sided political article without offering an opposite view. However, Blue sees this strategy not as a guarantee of the freedom of the press and of objectivity but as a pretext for not publishing his text.

p. 19 **5**

1. Conventions, Common Law, Acts of Parliament, European Union Law and ancient documents
2. It was in 1215 that the Magna Carta ensured the right to justice and protection against imprisonment without lawful reason and reliable witnesses.

3. Habeas Corpus is the Latin translation for "You have the body" which means that one is innocent until proven guilty, i. e. nobody could be imprisoned without lawful reason and prisoners were ensured the right to trial.
4. At that time, the King was considered to be the representative of God on earth, which meant he was the law and could decide everything without any further legitimization. The Magna Carta and Habeas Corpus Act protected people against the abuse of power by the King.
5. A constitutional monarchy means that the monarch rules by the grace of Parliament and not by the grace of God. The monarch is thus bound by laws. The British constitutional monarchy was founded in 1689 after the Glorious Revolution.
6. Written by Jefferson in 1776, declared the colonies' independence from England and affirmed the concept of inalienable rights.
7. Translation: Sie sind von ihrem Schöpfer mit gewissen unveräußerlichen Rechten ausgestattet ... zur Sicherung dieser Rechte sind Regierungen unter den Menschen eingesetzt, die ihre rechtmäßige Autorität aus der Zustimmung der Regierten herleiten.
Explanation: In contrast to so-called God-given rights that British monarchs ruling a hierarchical society claimed, American patriots referred to natural rights that ensure equality for all men. The citizens of a country have the right to choose their government who is responsible to them. As the British mother country and its king and government did not rule the American colonies according to these demands, the American Congress decided to become independent from Britain.
8. Thomas Jefferson in 1776 and George Washington in 1787
9. Amendment means "Zusatzartikel".
10. Rights ensured by the American Constitution and its amendments are freedom of religion, speech, peaceful assembly, the right to equal justice and security of citizens, the abolition of slavery, the right to vote irrespective of color, race and sex.

6 p. 20

(1) remember; (2) was coming; (3) walked; (4) had just heard; (5) was; (6) said; (7) crossed; (8) had been punched; (9) was trying; (10) had hurt/was hurting; (11) asked; (12) was; (13) said; (14) turned; (15) walked; (16) is; (17) was/has been built; (18) revels; (19) shows; (20) understood; (21) to be paid; (22) could/can; (23) (had) warned; (24) (had) urged; (25) spoke/had spoken; (26) honor/have honored; (27) have never listened; (28) is/has been; (29) are going; (30) have suffered; (31) have been

7 p. 21

a. 1i; 2d; 3g; 4f; 5j; 6c; 7l; 8a; 9e; 10h; 11b; 12k

b. (1) putting; (2) talking; (3) gathering; (4) setting; (5) raising; (6) advertising; (7) organizing; (8) reminding; (9) transporting; (10) polling

8 p. 22

a. cf. Students' Book, pp. 70–71

b. (Example)
I have endangered
the world around me.
But I have brought liberty
by reducing waste.

9

p. 23

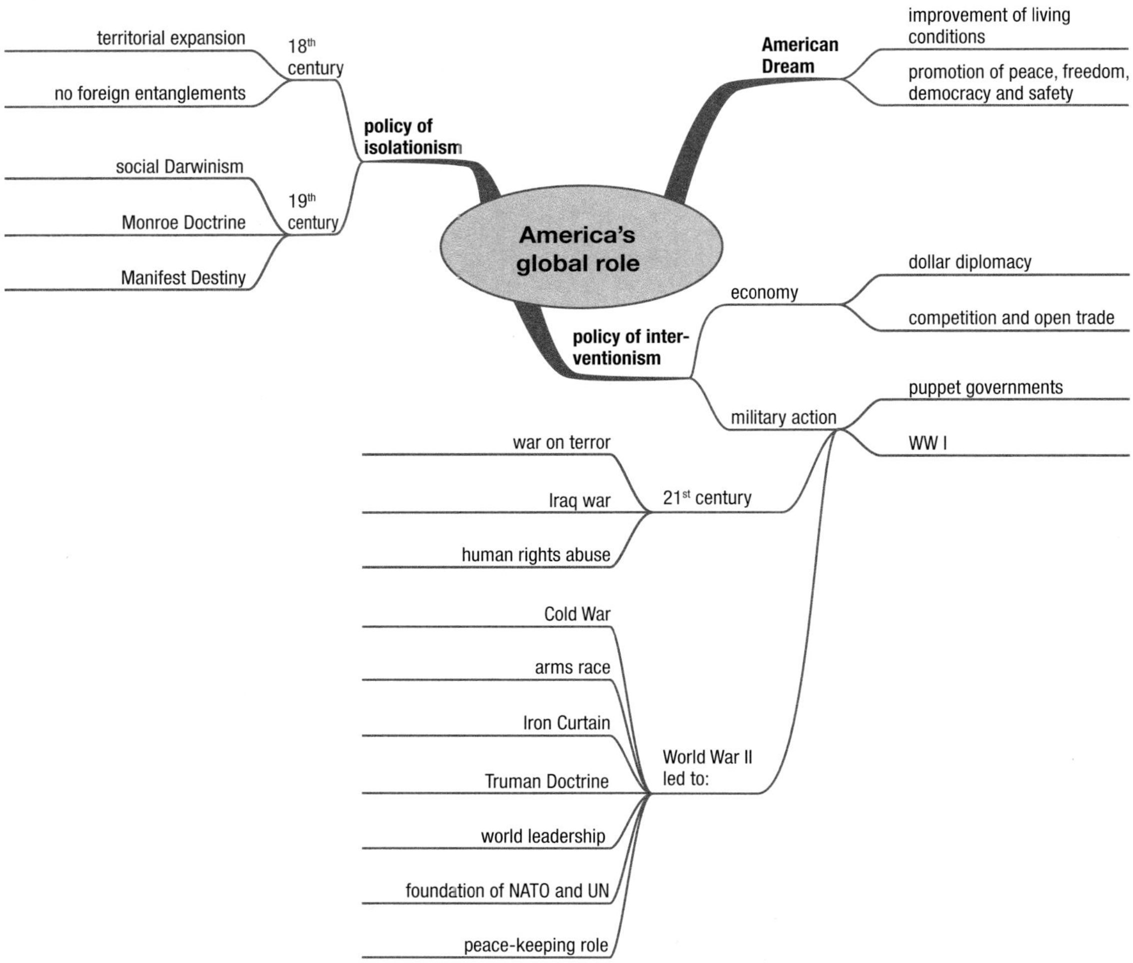

10

p. 24

a. The photo shows a stout person, probably a man, in a red shirt and with a **quadrangular hood** drawn completely over his head. The hood is made of **dark blue cloth** with white stars on it and it stands for the **US flag**. The photo is taken as a **medium shot** but attention is mostly drawn to the **enveloped head** that **covers** nearly two thirds of the photo.

b. The image has to do with the **anti-terror policy** of the USA and the **Iraq war**. It refers to the situation in **detention camps** like Guantànamo where **prisoners** were **tortured** by US **soldiers**. Such **prisoners** had their eyes covered by hoods and were **treated like animals** on a chain. The photo alludes to this **violation of human rights**.
The hood represents the USA and the red colour of the shirt may stand for blood as a **symbol of violence** and **torture**.
The title has a double meaning. On the one hand, the word star" represents the US flag and on the other hand, the title "Star Gazing" could also be understood as a criticism of Americans who are more interested in stars smiling from magazines than in political issues and Bush's war in Iraq. With this image, the audience is shocked by another, more political kind of "anti-star".

c. The photo touches me because it depicts unmistakably and without any words what happened in the **detention camps** during the **Iraq war**. The use of symbols such as the US flag and the form of the hoods worn by prisoners were well-chosen by the photographer. Everybody can understand the message of the photo although the title may be a bit too difficult to be deciphered appropriately.

d. The US flag stands for American core values such as life, liberty, the pursuit of happiness. It symbolizes the American Dream of unlimited possibilities.

Rivals – Allies – Friends

1 p. 26

(1) unification; (2) produced; (3) the best possible; (4) medium-sized; (5) limited; (6) significance; (7) citizens; (8) divided country enjoyed; (9) prosperity and consumption; (10) proclaimed; (11) nations; (12) "partners in leadership"; (13) gathered; (14) express their grief; (15) unconditional solidarity; (16) administration; (17) disregard; (18) seized; (19) trial; (20) a lawyer; (21) violation; (22) severely; (23) thoughts, ideas; (24) major; (25) cooperation

2 p. 26

1. Use of idiomatic phrases: lips are curled to pillory – *um anzuprangern*; "peens" or Euroweenies – *Eurowürstchen*; dissolved in a lukewarm bath of ... postmodern fudge – *haben sich in ... Spielchen verloren*; to jeer from the sidelines – *von den Zuschauerrängen johlen*; limp-wristed pansies – *tuntige Schwule = warme Brüder*
2. Use of fillers: often – *zu oft erweisen sie sich als*
3. Change of word types and phrases: a level of irritation – *Gereiztheit*; in the patriotic service – *Dienst für das Vaterland*
4. Omission of information: Europeans are ... hypocritical, disunited, duplicitous *heuchlerisch, zerstritten (doppelzüngig);* the emotional leitmotif – *das Leitmotiv*
5. Change of word order: They spend ... instead of ... – *statt für ... geben sie ihre Euros für ... aus*
6. Change of singular and plural: leitmotifs ... are resentment ... are irritation ... – *Leitmotiv ist Groll, ... Gereiztheit*
7. Change of passive into active sentences: A study should be written – *wäre eine Untersuchung wert*; the current stereotype is easily summarized – *Europäer gelten als ...*
8. Change of noun phrase into verbal phrase: even higher than the last memorable peak – *übertrifft die letzte Verstimmung*
9. Rendering participial constructions: polities destined to – *politische Gebilde, die ausersehen sind ...;* standing tall – *aufrecht*; resentment mingled with envy – *mit Neid durchsetzter Groll*
10. Personal → impersonal: Virtually everyone I spoke to – *Wenn von Europa die Rede ist ...;* I discovered, used in the form – *findet auch ... Verwendung*

3 p. 28

a.

adjective	opposite	noun
tolerant	intolerant	tolerance
sociable	unsociable	sociability
straightforward	reserved, indirect	straightforwardness
understanding	unsympathetic, intolerant	understanding
human	inhuman	humanity
fair	unfair	fairness
respectful	disrespectful	respectfulness
balanced	unbalanced, imbalanced	balance
outspoken	reticent, shy, reserved	outspokenness
cooperative	uncooperative	cooperation

b. Tolerant countries have room even for intolerant people.
Sociable people find friends everywhere. Get together.
Being straightforward means telling the truth – and accepting it when it's told. It's a chance to build our future.

p. 29 **4**

a. America:

Unschuld: innocence (foundation of a new country/nation)
Materialismus: materialism (praise of consumerism)
Erfolgsstreben: pursuit of success (American Dream)
Gleichheitsdenken: egalitarianism (Declaration of Independence and Bill of Rights)
Zukunftsoptimismus: believing/faith in the future
Mobilität: mobility (no word for "Heimat")
Identitäts- und Wurzellosigkeit: lack of identity and roots (no historical past)
Jugendkult: worship of youth (beauty surgery)
Freiheitsstreben: pursuit of freedom and liberty
Puritanismus: puritanism (attitude to sex, nakedness, body hair)
Aggressivität gegenüber der Natur: aggressive stance towards nature (lack of ecological thought)
Kreativität: (scope for) creativity (and free-thinking) (creativity is more important than social networking)
offene Gesellschaft: liberal and open society (chances for everybody who is willing to work hard)

Europe:

Erfahrung: experience and knowledge (due to a historical past and traditions)
Kultur: culture (multicultural Europe)
Sicherheitsstreben: need for security (exaggeration of the welfare state)
Klassenbewusstsein: class consciousness (social classes are more important than personal performance)
Traditionsbewusstsein: sense of tradition
Verwurzelung: desire for deep roots (to own one's house is a top wish of people)
Erstarrung im Überkommenen: mental inflexibility (people buy their house and do not move out and change)
Altersverehrung: respect for the older generation
Autoritätsgläubigkeit: blind obedience to authority (*Beamtentum*, civil service)
Lebensgenuss: enjoyment of life (consumption of beer at the age of 16 and of alcohol at 18)
Streben nach Harmonie zwischen Natur und Kultur: desire to balance nature and culture
Bildungsbürgertum: intellectual bourgeoisie/snobbery (social class is important and an appropriate network to make a career)
geschlossene Gesellschaft: conservative and closed society (fewer chances for children with a poor background)

b. Individual answers are expected.

Distinctly Canadian – I Wonder What They Are

p. 30 **1**

Dear boys and girls in Canada,

Thank you very much for the nice parcel my teacher gave me yesterday. I went home <u>pushing</u> my bike uphill because the parcel was so heavy! My mum <u>being</u> at work when I got home, we didn't open the parcel until late in the evening. <u>Sitting</u> at the kitchen table <u>doing</u> my homework, I couldn't concentrate because I desperately wanted to know what was in the parcel. It lay on the sofa <u>looking</u> really tempting but I had made up my mind to wait for mum and open it with her. With Dad <u>serving</u> as a soldier somewhere in France, it is only the two of us at the moment. Mum often lies in bed <u>crying</u> but I was sure she wouldn't cry this night. I knew she would be happy because of all the things you had sent us. We are lucky still <u>living</u> in our own home. Many houses have been bombed during the Blitz. <u>Having lost</u> everything, these people have to stay with relatives or even with people they don't know at all.

Mum feeling very hungry and tired when she came home from work, we sat down to dinner immediately. But then, kneeling in front of the sofa, we cut through the strings of the parcel. What lovely things you've got in Canada! The corduroy trousers are a little too big but I can wear them using a belt. With Dad not being at home at the moment, we will give the beautiful shirt to granddad. It all felt like Christmas and lying in bed, I dreamt of a shop full of corduroy trousers and Viyella shirts! Thanks very much again. People in Canada are very nice and very generous. Our teacher says you're helping us because, being all part of the British Empire, we must stick together, especially in times of hardship and war. When the war is over, I will visit your wonderful country. I'm looking forward to this.

Best wishes,
Sarah Brown from England

2 p. 31

a. eligibility requirements: *Voraussetzungen für die Berechtigung (zur Staatsbürgerschaft)*; dual citizenship: *doppelte Staatsbürgerschaft;* naturalized citizen: *eingebürgerter Einwanderer;* eligible immigrant: *berechtigter Einwanderer;* permanent residence: *dauernder Aufenthalt*

b. Most easily people can become Australian citizens. Only 2 years of permanent residence and an understanding of basic English are required. Also Canada's requirements are relatively low in comparison to the United States and the United Kingdom. Reasons seem to be that both Canada and Australia are countries with a small population. They have an interest in the immigration of qualified people. The number of naturalized citizens among eligible immigrants is quite high in these countries.

3 p. 32

a. 1g; 2h; 3f; 4b; 5j; 6i; 7c; 8d; 9a; 10e
1. to drive so. up the wall – *jdn. wahnsinnig machen*
2. to jump for joy – *vor Freude jubeln*
3. to be out of touch with sth. – *nicht mehr auf dem Laufenden sein*
4. to give sb. food for thought – *Stoff zum Nachdenken geben*
5. sth. works like magic – *es läuft wunderbar*
6. to be one's bread and butter – *seinen Lebensunterhalt verdienen*
7. to put one's foot in it – *ins Fettnäpfchen treten*
8. to be in dire straits – *in einer ernsten Notlage sein*
9. to carry the can – *den schwarzen Peter haben*
10. to come down to earth with a bang – *mit einem großen Knall auf den Boden der Tatsachen zurückkommen*

b. (1) are/were really out of touch with; (2) was Maria Campbell's bread and butter; (3) was really in dire straits; (4) made her come down to earth with a bang; (5) carry the can; (6) drove Maria up the wall; (7) it gave her food for thought; (8) worked like magic; (9) put her foot in it; (10) jump for joy

4 p. 33

The chart given is a pie chart that provides information about the minorities population in Toronto. Nearly half of the whole population comes from more than ten different minorities. The largest minorities are the Chinese and South Asian people with about 15 percent each. Then, black people reach a considerable percentage of more than 10 percent of Toronto's population. Smaller but visible minorities are Filipinos, West Asians, Arab people, Latin Americans, Koreans, and Southeast Asians. Are they Canadians? We do not know but the requirements from immigrants who want to become Canadian citizens are relatively low. One can suppose that most of these peoples have already become Canadians or they have applied for citizenship.

All in Society – I Wonder Who We Are

p. 34 **1**

a. Possible beginnings of answers:

1. e.g. "Yes, I see your point, but they can also promote healthy eating if you fill them with the right kind of things."
2. e.g. "That's true. Even Herr Schäuble, the former Minister of the Interior, has called for Germans to see Germany as an immigration country."
3. e.g. "Yes, sorry, you're right. The 1966 match is the one that we almost won!"
4. e.g. "He's dead right! And I think school should not start before 9 am so we can get enough sleep."
5. e.g. "Well, actually, there is evidence which refutes the effectiveness of capital punishment as a deterrent."
6. e.g. "Yes, I didn't take that into account. There are different laws in every state."

p. 35 **2**

1. If the governors hadn't decided positively, my future wouldn't look as bright as it does now.
2. If I keep on wearing my headscarf, I might encounter some difficulties in public.
3. I will be considered a threat to the British way of life unless I start eating ham and eggs for breakfast.
4. My family would be disappointed if they learned I haven't been given British citizenship.
5. If I hadn't come to this office, I would have never been told the good news.
6. Being called a threat to civilization is hard to understand unless you suffer from a lack of self-respect.
7. If I stopped living according to my religion, I would deny an important part of my personality that has been shaped by it.
8. Now I can start a career like British women, provided there are enough appropriate jobs I can apply for.
9. If still lived in Pakistan, I would lead a completely different life.

p. 35 **3**

1. They **were seen** as guest workers by the British, too.
2. Authorities **grant** an immigration permit to those immigrants whose ...
3. Authorities **assign** work permits to skilled immigrants who have skills ...
4. ... that each group of immigrants **is assimilated** into American society ...
5. The idea of assimilation **has largely been replaced** by the ideas of cultural pluralism ...
6. Prominent sociologists more often **use** alternative models where ... to describe how cultures and ethnicities ...

b. Initially, a group **was formed** under one umbrella.

p. 36 **4**

a. In nineteen minutes, you can mow the front lawn, color your hair, watch a third of a hockey game. In nineteen minutes, you can bake scones or get a tooth filled by a dentist; you can fold laundry for a family of five.
Nineteen minutes is how long it takes the Tennessee Titans to sell out of tickets to the play-offs. It's the length of a sitcom, minus the commercials. It's the driving distance from the Vermont border to the town of Sterling, New Hampshire.
In nineteen minutes, you can stop the world, or you can just jump off it. In nineteen minutes, you can get revenge.
from *Nineteen Minutes* by Jodi Picoult. London, Hodder & Staughton, 2008, p. 5

b. (1) superior court judge – *Richter am Berufungsgericht (in einigen Bundesstaaten der USA), vgl. Landesgericht*; (2) district court judge – *Richter am Bundesbezirksgericht, vgl. Amtsgericht*; (3) appointment – *Berufung*; (4) courtroom – *Gerichtssaal*; (5) prosecutors – *Staatsanwälte, Ankläger*; (6) legal system – *Rechtssystem/-wesen*; (7) guilty – *schuldig*

c.

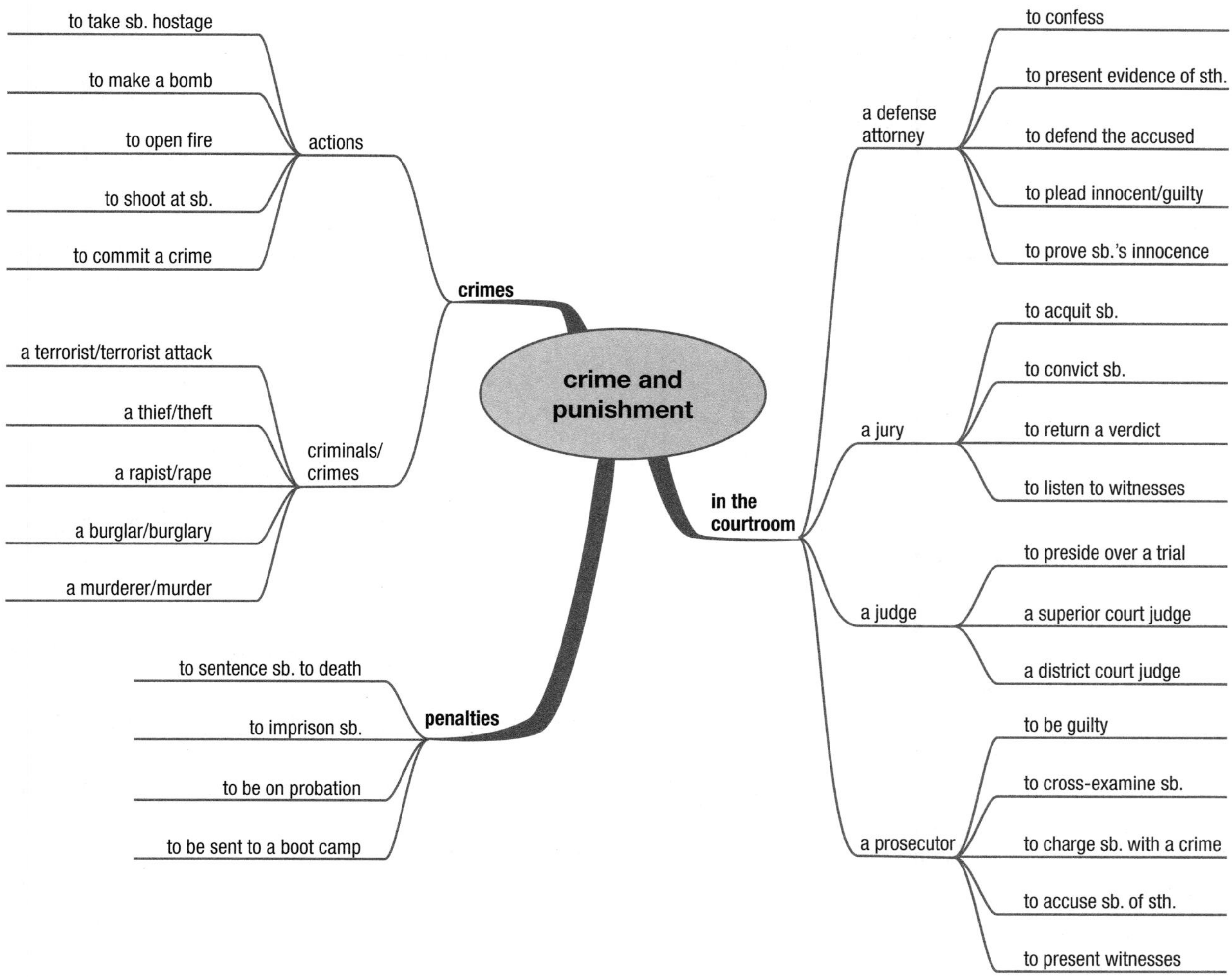

5 p. 38

(1) applied; (2) adult; (3) casual; (4) low-paid; (5) committing; (6) embodying; (7) glamour; (8) labelled; (9) features; (10) criticism; (11) ASBOs; (12) critics

6 p. 38

a. (1) Höchstgrenze; (2) zu versteuern, steuerpflichtig (3) Berufsbildung, Schulung; (4) Wiedereingliederungsmaßnahmen wie ABM, AfG; (5) anspruchsberechtigt; (6) freiwillige Versicherung; (7) Bruttogehalt; (8) Einkommensniveaus; (9) Berufsbiografie, vorherige Anstellungen; (10) unterschiedlich, wechselnd; (11) Beihilfen, Zuschüsse; (12) Pflichtversicherung; (13) innerhalb der 22 vorhergehenden Monate; (14) ceiling; (15) labour training or job reintegration (16) benefits; (17) runs/cuts; (18) eligible; (19) income; (20) preceding; (21) mandatory; (22) vary; (23) how long; (24) circumstances/cases; (25) Obligations; (26) available; (27) wage/salary/earnings/income; (28) amount

b.

A single, childless and unemployed 40-year-old man				
	How much?	**How long?**	**Obligations**	**Eligibility**
Denmark	90 % of gross wages up to $ 1,994 a month	four years	labour training, job reintegration programs	52 weeks (close to a year) of employment during last 3 years
France	57.4 % of gross salary up to $ 7,015 a month	23 months	efforts to find a new job	6 months of employment within preceding 22 months
German	60 % of net wages up to $ 2,018 a month	12 months	training programs	12 months of employment within last 3 years
United States	between $ 258 and $ 486 a week	16 to 26 weeks	acceptance of jobs paying 60 % of previous wage	minimum earnings within a 1 year period

p. 40 **7**

Jude reflected on how she felt when asked if she felt guilty. She confessed that the only thing that would make her reassess what she was doing would be if Harvey wasn't/hadn't been happy or seeing something going on in the nursery that she didn't like/hadn't liked.

Alexa said that the study didn't make her think again about anything she had done. She pointed out that Beth was very bright, very interactive, very helpful and added that in this day and age parents like her had to depend on childcare.

Simon wanted to know whether he was supposed to feel guilty. He pointed out that it was irksome that there had been no mention of fathers. He went on to say that he was confused: was it that a child would be better off with a parent, whether it was a mother or a father – in which case he agreed. Or would a mother be better than a father – in which case he couldn't agree.

Karina and Richard accused the r interviewer of suggesting that they should feel guilty. They confirmed that that sort of study made one feel uneasy about things one had no choice over. They admitted that for them nursery care was one of life's musts. They confessed that they didn't have the luxury of living on one wage.

p. 40 **8**

lower class	middle class	upper class
blue-collar worker	white-collar employee	title
GCSE	university degree	family background
council flat	semi-detached house	landowner
terraced house	salatariat (→ salary)	Oxbridge
trade-union member	self-employed	public school
welfare	suits and bowler hats	stately home
regional accent	common accent	posh accent
fish and chips	conformist life	political privileges
vote Labour Party	respectability	exclusivity
'Us'	('Them')	'Them'

9 p. 41

a.
to have a rough go: to experience hard times, to encounter difficulties
to be guide and a mentor: to help and give advice
to be more inclined to: to be more willing to
to put in place: to establish, to introduce
to take time off: to stop working and stay at home for a certain period of time
to be entitled to: to have the right to
to negotiate: to deal with, to cope with
to be eyed: to be watched or observed

b. 1d; 2d; 3b; 4d (and b); 5b; 6a

Going Global

1 p. 42

a. The cartoon shows two native Americans dressed in traditional clothes, each of them carrying a bow and quiver containing three, respectively two, arrows. Both are standing on a ledge and watching a covered wagon making its way through the prairie. The native American on the left is pointing at the covered wagon below and commenting on the ongoing expansion of the West by settlers. He considers the settlers to be intruders who are flooding the land and outnumbering the natives. He also states the natives' powerlessness and warns the other native American not to hire any of the aliens if he doesn't want to be fined. The cartoon is about the growing numbers of illegal aliens coming to the U.S. and the problems the U.S. is having in finding ways to deal with them.

b. Considering body language and the statement made, the two native Americans seem pretty harmless and passive; they are merely watching the scene. They aren't athletic and it seems as if they weren't intending to use their weapons. Besides, the number of arrows is very limited. The one with three arrows in his quiver may be considered to be in charge as he is aware of the ongoing development and the natives' powerlessness; in addition, he can forbid the other native from hiring newcomers and impose fines in case his rules are not obeyed.
The cartoonist is making illegal immigration the subject of this cartoon. On the one hand, putting a modern-day statement into a native American's mouth who is watching settlers in the days of the opening up of the West creates a humorous effect, as the viewer is reminded of the fact that the U.S.A. today is the result of immigration, very often against the natives' will. In other words, today's illegal immigrants are trying to do the same as the settlers did, thus provoking the same reactions among the natives. On the other hand, the two native Americans can be taken for the U.S. administration and the American people. The helplessness of the administration in view of the tides of illegal aliens is made a subject as well as Americans making use of this illegal, but cheap workforce. As the administration seems to be incapable of stopping illegal immigration, it tends to make the situation for illegal aliens in the U.S. as hard as possible, by threatening possible employers with fines in the hope of making the illegal aliens return to their native countries.
All in all, the cartoonist wants to draw attention to the problematic situation; he also asks for sympathy with illegal immigrants as they are driven by reasons that are entirely American.

c. I like this cartoon because it draws revealing parallels between two different periods of time.

2 p. 42

(1) foreign; (2) legal; (3) undocumented; (4) employment; (5) simply; (6) temporary worker program; (7) job offer; (8) be eligible; (9) return; (10) reasonable; (11) aliens; (12) expired; (13) enforce; (14) tough; (15) permanently; (16) incentives; (17) credit; (18) portion; (19) native; (20) business

3 p. 44

a. cf. Students' Book, p. 156

b. 1p; 2j; 3g; 4f; 5h; 6b; 7c; 8i; 9d; 10e; 11m; 12a; 13l; 14o; 15k; 16n

c.

1. Having reduced ... (= perfect participle instead of an adverbial clause of reason or adverbial clause of time) → As/Since they (have) reduced their hours, more and more workers see their chances .../After they have reduced their hours, ...

2. As their bosses don't take them seriously anymore, ... (= adverbial clause of reason) → With their bosses not taking them seriously anymore, ... (participle construction with subject of its own; without "with" a rather formal construction)

3. Lacking the confidence or the knowledge to introduce flexible or part-time working, ... (= present participle instead of an adverbial clause of reason or manner) → As/Since they lack the confidence or the knowledge to introduce flexible or part-time working, ...

4. ... published ... (= past participle instead of a relative clause) → ... that/which was published ... moving away from 'presenteeism' ... (= present participle instead of a relative clause) → ... who are moving away ...

5. Realizing the advantages for business and staff morale ... (= present participle instead of adverbial clause of reason or time) → As/Since they realize the advantages for business and staff morale, .../When they ...

p. 45 **4**

a. This diagram is based on data from the International Labor Organization, DECD. It provides information about the situation of working women in different countries. The diagram consists of two different parts: in the first part, it informs the reader about women as part of the labour force and women working in decision-making positions; in the second part, the percentage of male and female part-time work is compared.

The bars in the first diagram clearly show that women in all of the countries compared (U.S., U.K., Sweden, Germany, the Netherlands, Italy) form a large part of the labour force, with percentages ranging from between 37% and 47%. With regard to women holding a decision-making position, however, the respective countries vary significantly: whereas in the U.S. we find 45% of women in high positions, there are only 19% of them in comparable positions in Italy. In the other countries, the percentage varies relatively consistently between 24% and 33%.

One conclusion that can be drawn is that, in general, women in the countries studied work in lower positions than men, but that there are notable differences in the respective countries with regard to the number of women holding a higher position.

In the second part of the diagram, the U. S., the EU, Canada, Japan and Australia are compared with respect to men and women employed in part-time work. It is clearly shown that in all countries mentioned, men represent a relatively small share of part-time work, the percentages ranging from 8% in the U.S. to 16% in Australia, whereas the percentage of women working part-time ranges from 19% in the U.S. to 41% in Australia and 42% in Japan. This indicates a very different attitude towards equality of sexes and responsibility for the family in the given countries. To sum it up, one can say that equal rights for women in the world of work are still far from being achieved.

b. The Myth of Women's Equality in Europe

For all the myths of equality that Europe tells itself, the Continent is by and large a woeful place for a woman who aspires to lead. According to a paper published by the International Labor Organization, women account for 45 percent of high-level decision makers in America, including legislators, senior officials and managers across all types of business. In the UK, women hold 33 percent of those jobs. In Sweden they hold 29 percent. Germany comes in at just under 27 percent, and Italian women hold a pathetic 19 percent of power jobs.

It is not that European women are stuck in the house. After all, women make up 57 percent of the EU 15's workforce. The real problem is that Europe has been consistently unable to tap the highest potential of its female workers, who represent half of the college graduates in most countries. Women, it seems, can have a job – but not a high-powered career.

c. Frauen in Europa sind in Führungspositionen unterproportional repräsentiert.

5 p. 46

(1) globalisation; (2) phenomenon; (3) new; (4) centuries; (5) economy; (6) global; (7) G8 (8); new; (9) changes; (10) world trade; (11) degree; (12) kind; (13) telecommunications; (14) developing; (15) raw; (16) products; (17) developing; (18) Internet; (19) financial; (20) monetary

6 p. 47

a.

① The 1st cartoon shows several steps in the process of evolution passing from ape via anthropoid ape and Stone Age man, to early man carrying a club to *homo sapiens*; however, a latest evolutionary step has been added: a state-of-the-art robot replacing man as the most highly developed species. In short, man is no longer the crown of evolution.

② This cartoon shows the development of the typical English gentleman with a bowler hat, who is very often considered to be the embodiment of a civilized human being, but is descended from rather primitive ancestors, e. g. Vikings, who were notorious raiders, cavemen, and before that, from monkeys. The only feature connecting them is their grim facial expression, aka "stiff upper lip".

③ The 3rd cartoon depicts evolution from fish via amphibians and land animals to early man and modern man. In this case, security checks with metal detectors and x-ray scanners in public places are the endpoint of human evolution.

④ This cartoon shows a feminist view on the process of evolution with women being the crown of evolution.

b.

① From ape to man to robot sapiens
② The English gentleman – the crown of civilization
③ "Anything to declare, Mr. Just-came-out-of-the-sea?"
④ The evolution of the intelligent being

c.

similarities	differences
The process of evolution is depicted in slightly differing versions.	The single elements of the processes vary in number.
There is a starting point and a final point that is reached at the end.	In some cartoons, the emphasis is put on different processes, e. g. biological and historical ones.
The posture of the depicted (human) beings changes from stooping to more erect.	The dynamics of the developments are underlined in some cartoons by upward movements.
The last elements of the depicted evolutionary processes are inappropriate and therefore provoke a reaction in the viewer.	The caricatures were drawn by two different cartoonists, an advertisement designer and a pupil.

Cartoon 1: With A.I. (artificial intelligence) robots representing the latest evolutionary step, man is no longer the most highly developed species.
Cartoon 2: Even though the British gentlemen is often considered the embodiment of a civilized human being, his ancestry is much less cultivated and civilized.
Cartoon 3: Compulsory security checks mark the current endpoint of evolution.
Cartoon 4: Women are the crown of evolution.

7 p. 48

a. (1 e) to hold an opinion; (2 j) to keep a promise; (3 h) to encounter difficulties; (4 g) to spark a debate; (5 f) to raise hopes; (6 m) to carry out research; (7 d) to acknowledge a fact; (8 c) to tackle a problem; (9 b) to apply methods; (10 a) to cure a disease; (11 n) to come down with an infection; (12 i) to undergo a treatment; (13 k) to be given an anaesthetic; (14 l) to be on antibiotics

b.

1. Scientists often encounter difficulties when, in carrying out research, they apply methods that society doesn't regard as ethically justifiable.
2. In the field of genetic engineering, it often happens that hopes are raised in patients that, unfortunately, are later crushed.
3. Ill people on antibiotics, often come down with a secondary infection.
4. In order to cure diseases successfully, scientific research has to be carried out.
5. Before undergoing treatment, patients need to be examined carefully.
6. Scientists often hold the opinion that a full anaesthetic should only be given in exceptional cases.

p. 49 **8**

a. Disposal of Old Electrical & Electronic Equipment (Applicable in the European Union and other European countries with separate collection systems)
This symbol on the product or on its packaging indicates that this product shall not be treated as household waste. Instead it shall be handed over to the applicable collection point for the recycling of electrical and electronic equipment. By ensuring this product is disposed of correctly, you will help prevent potential negative consequences for the environment and human health, which could otherwise be caused by inappropriate waste handling of this product. The recycling of materials will help to conserve natural resources. For more detailed information about recycling of this product, please contact your local city office, your household waste disposal service or the shop where you purchased the product.

b. Disposal of Old Electrical & Electronic Equipment (Applicable in the European Union and other European countries with separate collection systems)
Look for this symbol on the product or on its packaging. It tells you that the product must not be treated as household waste. Instead, you must hand it over to the appropriate collection point for the recycling of electrical and electronic equipment. If you handle the waste of this product appropriately, you will help prevent negative consequences for the environment and human health. The recycling of materials will help to conserve natural resources. For more detailed information about the recycling of this product, please contact your local city office, your household waste disposal service or the shop where you bought the product.

p. 50 **9**

a.
- theme: the adverse effects of obesity
- the chain-reaction: obesity is humorously portrayed as the root cause of a whole host of mainly environmental problems – global warming, killing endangered species, nuclear proliferation, depletion of the rain forest

b.
- **Caption and text:**
  – ~~Obvious~~/obviously, the clear/~~clearly~~ yet blunt/~~bluntly~~ and simplistic/~~simplistically~~ caption claims that obese people are to blame for everything bad in/~~on~~ the world.
  – The extensive use of "scientific words" and language is meant to give the impression of/~~for~~ objectivity and clarity.
- **Topical relevance:**
  – Obesity is widely seen as a ~~mayor~~/major threat to/~~for~~ first world ~~economys~~/economies and health systems.
- **Humorous effect is created through:**
  – the juxtaposition of the seemingly/~~seeming~~ "objective" and "scientific" ~~to~~/with the truly/~~true~~ trivial, e. g. the overexaggeration ~~of~~/in the "scientific" claim made in the caption,

- the unimportant/~~inimportant~~ and ludicrous factors included in the "scientific" flowchart (popping button, tipping box, etc.),
- the dramatic extent of the problem/~~the problem's dramatic extent~~,
- the simplistic causal ~~modell~~/model,
- the use of clichés, e. g./~~f. ex.~~ the cream cake, the ridiculous labels, or
- the evil spy with dark sunglasses.

- **The cartoonist's attitude and intention:**
  - The cartoon includes all the topical problems and nightmares ~~who~~/that humanity faces in one cartoon and links them ~~in~~/to one trite model.
  - Hyperbole is used to trivialize the matter: Although the matters addressed are definitely relevant to/~~for~~ the world, the method of presenting them trivializes them.
  - All that possibly reveals that the cartoonist is fed up with/~~about~~ hearing all the buzz words repeated by/~~from~~ the doomsday prophets.

10 p. 51

a. (1) burning fossil fuels; (2) deforestation; (3) rice fields; (4) aerosols; (5) greenhouse gases; (6) incoming sunlight; (7) reflected sunlight; (8) trapped infrared energy; (9) ice and snow; (10) reflected sunlight; (11) escaping infrared energy → global warming

b.

to heat up sth.
eyes closed
to crank
a crank
suit and tie
earth
man
spit
cow
to roast
exhaust
firewood
gases
factory/factories
chimney
livestock
cars
plane

The message of the cartoon is that it is mankind that is responsible for global warming.

c. (1) will have/would have; (2) Launching/Having launched; (3) said; (4) was already changing/had already changed/had already been changing; (5) would continue; (6) would be growing/was growing; (7) will have shifted; (8) resembling; (9) moving; (10) will become

11 p. 53

a. Game Boy?
Being a child is no children's game. Children have the right not to have to become soldiers.

Terre des hommes
Help for children in need

Game over. Not for John. And he does not have an extra life, either. War is not a game. Worldwide, more than 300,000 child soldiers have to fght on some warfront. Death and destruction leave deep traces in the souls of these children. They need our help. For further information, call: 0541/7101-128

p. 53 **12**

a. 1d (a. 1776: Declaration of Independence; b. 1865: Assassination of President Lincoln and abolition of slavery; c. 1952: Coronation of Queen Elizabeth II); 2b; 3d; 4c; 5a; 6d; 7c

p. 54 **13**

1. anaphora, antithesis
2. parallelism, antithesis
3. simile
4. comparison, parallelism, antithesis
5. paradox, tautology
6. allusion (to Shakespeare line), extended metaphor
7. anaphora, repetition, antithesis
8. parallelism, alliteration, synecdoche/symbol
9. anaphora, paradox

p. 55 **14**

(1) focuses on; (2) refer to; (3) traditional; (4) process of dividing; (5) transferring; (6) government; (7) usually favour; (8) loose federations (to lose: *verlieren*); (9) can be achieved through movements; (10) its base (it's = it is); (11) put forward several arguments; (12) often goes along (adverb of frequency before verb); (13) Thus regionalism (zero-article with abstract nouns); (14) separation; (15) was demonstrated in the late 1980s

Culture – High and Low

p. 56 **1**

1. Text type: this text is an argumentative one as it focuses on the author's evaluation of an expensive piece of art.
2. Heading: the author arouses the reader's interest by juxtaposing two seemingly separate spheres, i. e. the religious and commercial ones.
3. Topic: the general topic of this text is the value of art in connection with the status of Damien Hirst.
4. Intention: the text draws the reader's attention to the ambivalent nature of modern art.
5. Structure: this text is divided into four paragraphs. In the first paragraph, the author describes Hirst's latest piece of art and points out the mixed reactions of the public to it ...
6. Author's attitude: from an intellectual point of view, the author discusses the multi-faceted issue in an openminded way.
7. Author's competence: the author is well informed about Hirst's art provocation and displays profound knowledge about the workings of the art market.
8. Author's argumentation: the author supports his arguments by using contrasts and quoting the artist.
9. Style: the author makes use of elaborated journalese, employing metaphorical language and many Latin terms.
10. Tone: the light-hearted and slightly smug tone is meant to entertain, inform and make the reader ponder about modern art.

p. 56 **2**

(1) Stuckism; (2) Abstract Expressionism; (3) Body Art; (4) Color Field; (5) Land Art; (6) Op Art; (7) Video Installation; (8) Pop Art; (9) Street Art; (10) Young British Artists (YBAs, Brit Art)

3 p. 57

1. His clear and simple art is a reaction to a world which is complex, chaotic, and dominated by visuals.
2. He collects deadwood and mud from the bank of the Severn river. The reasons are that you can make wonderful pictures from water and mud, and that he is still living there.
3. In America, there are too many places saying "no trespassing", and where you can get shot.
4. When he was a young art student, he was expelled from the West England College of the Arts during his final semesters, now he is a member of the Royal West England Academy of the Arts.
5. Discovering new and different places before coming back to the same place – but as a different person.

4 p. 58

Lots of contracted forms (haven't, you've, wasn't ...), positive statement (with rising intonation) as question (l. 8), rejoinder and ellipsis (ll. 10, 28, 74), interjection (l. 13), slang exclamation (l. 15), repetition (l. 26), fillers (l. 62), parallelism (l. 69), weak forms, vowel reductions, elisions: cf. Audio CD

5 p. 58

(1) issue/topic; (2) alter/transform; (3) forms/types; (4) harmful/detrimental to; (5) appreciate/cherish; (6) view/perspective; (7) pleasant/comfortable; (8) excellent/brilliant; (9) amusing/comical; (10) rapidly; (11) prompt/real-time; (12) instantly/immediately; (13) fascinating/thought-provoking; (14) researching/retrieving; (15) information; (16) notable/critical; (17) proceed/continue on; (18) employed/made use of; (19) harmful/detrimental to; (20) munching/wolfing; (21) sorts/forms; (22) realize/are aware; (23) appreciate; (24) believe/imagine; (25) more effortless/less demanding; (26) quality/high-brow; (27) major/principal; (28) teenagers/adolescents; (29) acquire/adopt; (30) proper/appropriate; (31) unusually/extremely; (32) undeniably/clearly; (33) conclude/summarize; (34) truly/evidently

6 p. 59

a.

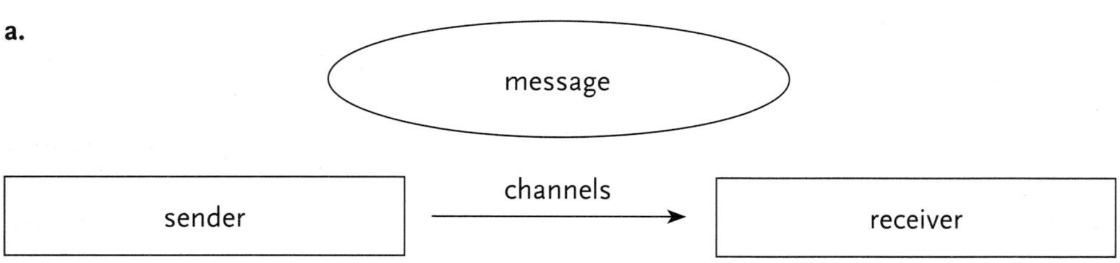

b.
feature film – audio-visual media, video installation – art media, website – hypermedia, newspaper – print media, radio – aural/oral media

c. • media literacy: refers to the process of accessing, analysing, evaluating and creating messages in various media.
• ideographic writing: is a writing method which uses graphic symbols to represent objects or ideas.
• information overload: refers to an excess amount of information being provided, making it difficult for the individual to process tasks.

d. *Medienkompetenz, Informationsüberflutung*

7 p. 60

a.
1. video sharing website
2. social networking
3. Wiki

4. podcast
5. blog

b.
1. ... represent different phenomena.
2. ... which you can gain entry to with the help of ...
3. ... invented/brought into use ...
4. ... intend to make working together easier ...
5. ... been degraded to a PR slogan.

p. 61 **8**

p. 61 **9**

... the **early** modern period of English ... The **Anglo**-Saxon vocabulary ... where **Latin and** Greek were given ... playing with **double** meanings ... Shall I compare thee to a **summer's** day?

p. 61 **10**

a. Comparing life to a play, Jaques describes the seven stages of man's life: infant, schoolboy, lover, soldier, justice, pantaloon, and second childhood.

b.
- the stage as a metaphor for life
- The seventh age is characterized as "second childishness and mere oblivion, sans teeth, sans eyes, sans taste, sans everything." Man becomes stupid and foolish like a child again.
  Without teeth, sight, taste, without any meaning in life, he becomes nothing, forgotten by the public.
- "The whining school-boy, with his satchel and shining morning face" is "creeping like snail unwillingly to school." As he does not like school, he walks "like a snail", i. e. very slowly in the hope of missing the first minutes of the lesson. (Other similes, i. e. comparisons introduced by *like* or *as*, are: "the lover, sighing like furnace", the soldier "bearded like the pard", ...)
- melancholy, pessimistic

p. 62 **11**

(1) think; (2) hairy; (3) laugh; (4) play; (5) inside; (6) night; (7) hot; (8) frisbee; (9) Juliet; (10) head; (11) star; (12) factory

p. 63 **12**

(1) Laying everybody low; (2) how about it; (3) a heart attack; (4) come around here; (5) from the start; (6) the time was wrong; (7) just the same; (8) one of your deals; (9) fall for; (10) thick and thin;

(11) we made love; (12) There's a place; (13) it's meant to be; (14) be in love; (15) keep the beat; (16) any time

13 p. 65

(1) according; (2) sitting; (3) asked; (4) handling; (5) made; (6) answering; (7) starring; (8) set; (9) confusing; (10) explaining; (11) adding; (12) hearing; (13) being murdered; (14) asking; (15) written; (16) seeing; (17) believing; (18) going; (19) taken; (20) dying

14 p. 66

Watching Shakespeare plays can be more dangerous than one may assume. The London Globe Theatre has issued a health warning after four people collapsed during a production of *Titus Andronicus*. The Bard's bloodiest play shows scenes of rape and murder. Its most famous scene comes when the Queen is served a pie filled with the cooked flesh of her own sons. But it was the horrific scene in which Lavinia has her hands cut off and tongue cut out that proved too gruesome for the groundlings, the audience members who stand in the Yard.

15 p. 66

a.

English word	English definition	German equivalent
sonnet	poem of 14 lines	*Sonett*
stanza	part of a song	*Strophe*
playwright	person who writes plays	*Dramatiker*
punch line	The last few words of a humorous story, joke	*Pointe*
to resemble	to look like	*ähneln*
to brag	to show off	*angeben*
addressee	person who is addressed	*Adressat, Zielpublikum*
soliloquy	speaking one's thoughts aloud (without sb. else being present on stage)	*Monolog, Selbstgespräch*
weary	tired/sick of sth.	*überdrüssig*
satire	mocking sb./sth. in order to criticize it/them	*Satire*
romance	story about the love between two people	*Liebesgeschichte*
tights	long stockings fitting tightly over feet and legs	*Strumpfhose*
to tread (trod, trodden)	to set one's foot down	*gehen, treten*
supernatural	impossible to explain by natural causes	*übernatürlich*
ambition	a strong desire to achieve sth.	*Ehrgeiz*
at first sight	the first time that you look at sb./sth.	*auf den ersten Blick*
tragedy	play that ends sadly (often with the protagonist's death)	*Tragödie*
(infml.) to fall for	to be tricked into believing sth. which is not true	*hereinfallen*

English Around the World

p. 68 **1**

(1) pattern; (2) rapid; (3) slowing; (4) taking off; (5) decline; (6) primary; (7) steady; (8) reached; (9) majority; (10) peak; (11) represents; (12) studying; (13) cradle

A – D – B – C

p. 69 **2**

a.

1. true

2. false: As to the number of native speakers, English is No 3 – after Mandarin Chinese and Spanish.

3. true

4. false: A lingua franca is used by speakers who do not share a common mother tongue, e. g. an Italian and a German talk to each other by using English.

5. true

6. true

7. true

8. false: BBC English, which is the standard, used to be a dialect.

9. false: British English and American English are the two major branches, Australian English is a sub-type of British English.

10 true

p. 69 **3**

Raumbelegungsplan: It is a schedule that regulates the allocation of rooms, e. g. in schools/at universities.

Schienenersatzverkehr: It is the replacement or substitution of a regular train by buses or taxis due to line repairs.

Bundesverfassungsgericht: It is the highest court of appeal in Germany, like the Supreme Court in the US.

Jugendschutzgesetz: It is a law for the protection of young people in public.

Kostümzwang: to be or feel forced to wear fancy dress, especially for Carnival

Solidaritätszuschlag: an additional pay deduction to finance the rebuilding and economic redevelopment of the former East Germany

Vertretungsstunde: a lesson covered by a substitute teacher

Sperrstunde: official and legally-fixed closing time of restaurants, bars and pubs

p. 69 **4**

1. keen on/eager to have

2. different ethnic groups/societal norms and language varieties co-existing in a balanced environment

3. have been badly/deeply affected [...] conflicts/struggles concerning beliefs and attitudes

4. attendants and domestic workers who didn't get enough wages/salary for their work

5. to re-settle in the country/area/region where they originally came from

6. unpleasant/bitter/traumatic recollections/remembered incidents

p. 70 **5**

abbreviations: DJ, UN, exam (examination), gym (gymnasium), gas (gasoline)

affixation: dis-, non-, hyper-, mega-, ex-; -able, -al

back-formation: burgle (burglar), donate (donation), lase (laser), edit (editor), sightsee (sightseeing)

Moving On

1 p. 71

a.

A good application should ...	A good application should NOT ...
• be written in good, formal English. • be seen as your personal "business card" which can be your ticket to the job you desire. • contain a formal cover letter, in which you mention the reasons for applying, and include a CV and copies of important certificates as well as other references. • present a true estimation of your own knowledge and abilities. • give information about why you are the right person for this particular job. • be printed on high quality, white paper.	• contain mistakes. • overemphasize your own abilities or knowledge because this gives an arrogant impression. • include information or certificates which have nothing to do with the job. • be crammed with too much information so that it is difficult to read. • be too generic.

b.

Fritz Meyer
Schillerstr. 17
97074 Würzburg
Germany

Job Centre
4 Watt Street
Gosford NSW 2250
Australia

July 1, 2009

Dear Sir or Madam,

On the Internet I found your job offer for working as an au pair in an Australian family.

After finishing my final exams at school (Abitur), I would like to study social pedagogy at a German university. Before studying, I would like to spend some time abroad, working with children. As I have four younger siblings, I am used to living in a big family and helping my parents with the household chores.

I have read a lot about Australia and I am also taking English as a main subject for my final exams. Since I am very interested in getting an insight into Australian culture, I would appreciate the opportunity to live and work in an Australian family.

I look forward to hearing from you soon.

Yours faithfully,

Fritz Meyer

example of a CV: → Students' Book, Method Kit, p. 279